RUGBY UNION
THREEQUARTER PLAY
A GUIDE TO SKILLS, TECHNIQUES AND TACTICS

RUGBY UNION
THREEQUARTER PLAY
A GUIDE TO SKILLS, TECHNIQUES AND TACTICS

PETER JOHNSON
FOREWORD BY STUART LANCASTER

THE CROWOOD PRESS

First published in 2013 by
The Crowood Press Ltd
Ramsbury, Marlborough
Wiltshire SN8 2HR

www.crowood.com

British Library Cataloguing-in-Publication Data
A catalogue record for this book is available from the British Library.

ISBN 978 1 84797 395 5

Acknowledgements
The author would like to acknowledge the contributions of action
photographs from the following Premiership Academies: London Irish,
Bristol Rugby and Filton College, Leicester Tigers, Saracens and Oaklands
College, Gloucester Rugby and Hartpury College, London Wasps and
Henley College, Sale Sharks and Myerscough College, Worcester Warriors
and Worcester VIth Form College, Exeter Chiefs and Truro College. Thanks
also to Matt Sheratt of Bristol Rugby for his help on the chapter on the
Threequarter Line.

Typeset by Phoenix Typesetting, Auldgirth, Dumfriesshire

Printed and bound in India by Replika Press Pvt Ltd

CONTENTS

FOREWORD

by Stuart Lancaster

Understanding positional roles, the job that each player has to do on the field, is an important requirement for any coach. My experience of coaching in the Premiership, of being the RFU's Head of Elite Player Development and Head Coach of the England team has given me enough insight to say that Peter Johnson's book is a valuable resource for any coach or player.

I have known Peter for several years, when he was a Regional England Academy Manager from 2001 and since 2006 helping to organize the apprenticeship programme in the Premiership clubs.

This book looks at each position in the threequarter line and deals with the attributes and skills which are required for a player to fulfil that positional role. Peter then considers how a player can develop those skills to become more competent and effective.

As a player, you may already have great coaches helping you; however, you should be taking more responsibility for your own progress. You know how much time you want to devote to improving and how dedicated you are. As a coach, you want to help the players analyse their individual performances, suggest ways of improving their weaknesses, and then supervising that fault correction programme. This book can help the players become self-autonomous and coaches become more knowledgeable and helpful to their players.

Whether as a player or coach, I can highly recommend this book. Good luck with your future in rugby.

Stuart Lancaster
Level 5 Coach
2001 Academy Manager at Leeds Carnegie
2006 Director of Rugby, Leeds Carnegie
2008 Head of Elite Player Development for the Rugby Football Union and coach to the Saxons
2012 Head Coach England Rugby

CHAPTER I

INTRODUCTION

Core Skills

Every sport has a number of basic skills, with players being selected for a team because they demonstrate these abilities better than others. In rugby union, players are judged on their ability in the basic or core skills of handling, tackling, ball retention, kicking and evasion. In addition, they need to achieve a level of fitness that will allow them to complete their positional tasks throughout the game; they will need to be able to make correct tactical decisions with ball in hand; and they will need to be motivated by a sense of pride in their own performance.

At the highest level of the game, while the core skills requirements are such that any threequarter should be able to play in any position in the back line, there are still certain unique skills demanded of each position. This book examines the specific roles and responsibilities of each of the positions in the threequarters. It is quite likely these days that any back could play at Fly Half, but selectors will still be looking at which of those backs will make the best Fly Half and what will make him better able to fulfil that role than any of his fellow squad members. Success in match play is about getting the right player in the right position.

This book looks at what is required of the player in each position, and the essential specific skills that are distinctive to each position, with a heavy emphasis on the technical and tactical demands and how these can be developed. It aims to help coaches, players and anyone interested in developing an understanding of the role of the threequarters. For coaches and players, there are suggestions on how to develop the requisite positional skills on the training field, with skill practices for specific technical and tactical aspects, showing progressions into the game.

Strength and conditioning programmes are not discussed here but the physical skills for each position can be developed through game-related exercises and some examples are provided. The mental skills discussed are common to all positions but, due to the differing roles and responsibilities of each position, the emphasis changes. For example, decision-making is important for every position, but the Fly Half is required to take more decisions under pressure of time and space, and with a huge amount of cues to filter, than any other player on the pitch.

Each chapter on the role and responsibilities of each positional is divided into five elements: a checklist of positional skills and attributes; the specialist role; development of specialist technical and tactical skills; development of specialist physical skills; development of specialist mental skills. These are followed by two chapters on the mini units of the threequarter line – the midfield and back three – explaining how these operate together in attack and defence.

The final chapter gives advice on getting the whole threequarter line working together. Rather than describing the set piece moves, it

Ambition, attitude, achievement.

presents ideas on how back lines can be developed in an enjoyable way, with more game-related practice.

Ambition: 'Aspire to climb as high as you can dream.' Anon

Attitude: 'If it is to be, it is up to me.' Anon

Achievement: 'Unless you try to do something beyond what you have already mastered, you will never grow.' Anon

CHAPTER 2

THE SCRUM HALF (9)

Checklist of Positional Skills and Attributes

Technical
- Has a range of passes.
- Clears the ball quickly and accurately off either hand, from the ground and from the chest.
- Accurate kicker off either foot to relieve pressure and create attack options.
- Tackles aggressively to stop forward movement of player or ball.

Tactical
- Understands the lineout calls, back-row moves and back-line plays and when to use them.
- Has vision and ability to use blind-side.
- Makes the right tactical decisions – pass, kick or run.
- Communicates and organizes defensive screens with loose forwards and others, for example, Fly Half and Blind-side Wing

Physical
- Acceleration: shows speed off the mark and outpaces opponents. Explosive runner from base of scrums and phase plays (speed and strength).
- Power: drives through tackles as ball carrier and influences contact as tackler.
- Strength: is able to withstand contact without detriment to skill levels.
- High work rate: has endurance, is energetic, is a 'livewire'.
- Agility: outmanoeuvres opponents.

Mental
- Organizational and talking skills.
- Perky, cheeky, adventurous.
- Personal impact on game: has positive influence on team-mates, makes big plays, makes team-mates better.
- Mental toughness: rises to the occasion, has a killer instinct.
- Determined, competitive.
- Composure and self-discipline: in control of emotions and distractions, maintains discipline to team plan.
- Knowledge of the laws.
- A 'nose' for the ball.
- Good anticipation and ability to adjust to situations.

The Specialist Role of the Scrum Half

The Scrum Half is a key player in the team, performing a pivotal role as the link between the forwards and the backs. The position requires someone who is a leader with good communication skills, to boss the forwards in attack and defence; a decision-maker who decides when the ball is produced and what happens next; and a reader of the game, a tactician.

In the chain of command, the Scrum Half is the first decision-maker at the secondary phases. His field of vision is fairly narrow around the immediate vicinity of the centre of action, while the Fly Half has a broader view.

The Scrum Half may call for a runner from the forwards to take a short pass and crash into the channel close to the breakdown, but the Fly Half may over-rule the 9's call, because he can see an opportunity a bit further away from the breakdown, perhaps a gap in the midfield. The backs further out may in turn over-rule the Fly Half's call, if they see something on for themselves, perhaps an overlap.

As well as possessing the essential tactical and mental skills, a good Scrum Half must also be accomplished in a wide range of technical skills and have the physical attributes to cope with the robust nature of the position.

Ideally, the Scrum Half will be equally skilled off both the right and the left side. However, it is the case that much of the Scrum Half's activity goes from left to right, so it can be an advantage in the early years of a Scrum Half's career to be left-handed and right-footed. From scrums, the Scrum Half tends to use the left more often than the right hand, for example, when passing from left to right, but also when passing from right to left, when a pivot pass will often be used. This means that the body is between the ball and the opposing Scrum Half, preventing the possibility of interference. Generally, the only position where a right-handed pass would be made from set-piece play is from a lineout on the right side of the field. From breakdowns, the 9 has a choice.

The right foot is pointing at the receiver, thus getting the knee out of the way and opening up a passing channel.

Note the right foot: to get more length on the pass, many Scrum Halfs will generate more power by swinging the back foot behind them, creating a 'whiplash' effect.

Development of Specialist Technical and Tactical Skills

Passing from Set Pieces

Attacking Scrums

At an attacking scrum, the Fly Half has priority if the ball is required. If not, then the Scrum Half organizes a back-row move. An early call is desirable, and all the forwards should know their role in the planned move.

The most important skill of the Scrum Half is to pass quickly and accurately to the Fly Half. Quite simply, if this does not happen, the team's back line will fail to function. Every good back line is made by a good Scrum-Half pass. Speed and accuracy go together and neither a slow accurate pass, nor a fast in-accurate one, is acceptable to the Fly Half.

The length of the pass should also be taken into account. This will depend on the strength of the wrists and forearms and on getting into the right body position to prevent wind up and back swing.

The obvious advantage of a long pass from the Scrum Half is that it probably puts the Fly Half out of reach of the defending open-side flanker. However, one disadvantage of a long pass is that the outside backs have less space in which to operate. If, for example, the pass is 15 metres rather than 10 metres, that is 5 metres of space they have lost. A Scrum Half needs to be able to pass long, but he must always take into account the time a long pass takes to reach the receiver. Any 'loop' on the flight will give extra time for the defenders to

A. PASSING FROM BASE OF SCRUM

Activity	Key learning points

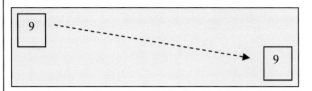

Static pass from ground 7 paces away
- Start with hands on ball.
- Progress to hands on knees

- Use wrists.
- Concentrate on hands.
- Ensure that follow-through is towards target.

Add a defender to cause pressure
- Both passer and defender start with hands on knees.
- Defender at right-angles to SH and 50cm away.
- As soon as passer makes a movement towards ball, defender can try to prevent pass.

- Avoid any wind-up.
- If too long with follow-through, passer has left his hands on ball too long.
- Hands end up on shoulder.

Without moving feet, pass a number of balls to a partner over a variety of ranges starting with 7m.

Extensions:
- Quick hands developed by quickly passing a number of balls to the FH, almost without looking. FH puts them down immediately because there should be another on its way.
- To eliminate wind-up, place ball next to a wall or table turned on its side so there is only enough room between the ball and object to put a hand.
- One-handed pass to develop wrists and fingers.

- Keep feet still.
- Maintain wide base and bent knees.
- Stay low between each pass.
- Back foot next to ball.
- Roll ball off fingertips.
- Vary the dominant hand.

Timed pass using 10 balls

Excellent	Less than 5 secs
Very good	5–6 secs
Good	6–7 secs
Average	7–8 secs
Improvement required	8+ secs

- Start to use 'peripheral vision' out of corner of eye.
- Communication by receiver to passer.

B. SCRUM BALL 8 and 9 and 10

Activity	Key learning points
■ 1 v 1 scrummaging. ■ 9 feeds scrum, ball is hooked and passed to FH. ■ 9 either loops outside 10 or receives an inside pass.	■ Communication between 8 and 9. ■ No. 8 distributes through feet on SH's signal. ■ Or lifts and breaks to the right to feed 9.
■ Ball at No. 8's feet. ■ 8 controls ball various ways (forwards, back, pick up). ■ 9 passes to 10 or breaks with 8. ■ Introduce an opposing 9 who becomes active when 8 or 9 touch the ball.	■ Or simulates a wheel and lifts and distributes ball with back to opposition.
■ Break from the base of a scrum	■ Try and stand the defender up and then go around him.

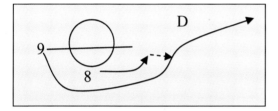

(Left) *A throw to the back of the lineout takes out the opposition back row and thus relieves the pressure on the Fly Half 's kicking option. The other lineout option achieving the same result is a catch at 4 and a subsequent drive pulls in the back row.*

come up to and drift on to the receiver. If a long pass will put a runner outside the defence, it must be flat and fast, and travel horizontally, and be run on to by a player going forward at speed.

Attacking Lineouts
At an attacking lineout, the Scrum Half is responsible for an early call. Is the call 'off the top' or drive or catch and give? If the plan is to get a Centre or Forward to go crashing

Continued on page 16

C. PASSING FROM THE LINE-OUT

Activity	Key learning points

Ball is distributed to SH off the ground

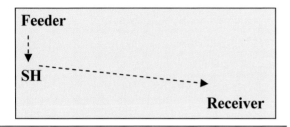

Passing from the line-out on the run

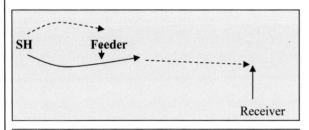

- Grasp the ball early.

- Pass the ball early.

- Pass from waist height.

- Avoid dropping the ball down too far (pendulum).

- If passing from left to right, try to receive ball level with left side of body to prevent wind-up.

- 2 throws to jumper 4 who feeds 9 in different ways:
  - off the top of the jump;
  - catch and driven and give off the ground;
  - catch and driven, ball presented on the ground.
- 9 passes to 10 – 2 and 8 oppose in pincer movement.

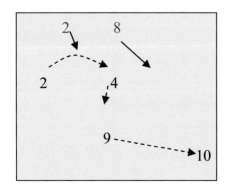

The ball is trapped under bodies and the Scrum Half has to go in to pull it out.

Note again the back foot. Although the Scrum Half gets more power and length on the pass, if his leg were following the ball, he would be off the blocks sooner and be getting to the next breakdown quicker.

Continued from page 13
into the opposition midfield, the 9 should aim for a flat pass to the Fly Half.

Decision-Making at Phase Play Attack

Scanning
One priority for the Scrum Half is to arrive quickly at the breakdown. Whilst approaching it, 9 should scan the areas immediately to the sides of the centre of the action to consider the way the defence is organized in width and depth. On approaching the breakdown, the 9 must talk to the forwards and either call a move involving them or let them know where the ball is going.

Shape of the Defence
If the defence is spread out in a single line of players, with little depth, then the Scrum Half can call for a runner from the forwards to drive at the defending line. If a runner can take out a single defender and off-load to a second runner, coming from depth and at speed, then the attacking team has got in behind the tackle line. If the defending players are bunched near the breakdown, the decision should be to move the ball wider to the Fly Half, who in turn decides the next point of attack.

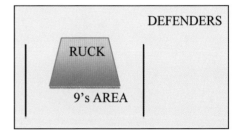

If passing to a forward off the edge of the ruck, the Scrum Half may have to take a

The ball should be pulled back, the player should step back and clear any groping hands to make space for the pass away.

Blue Scrum Half approaching the breakdown with his head up.

couple of paces sideways so that the pass is made to a forward on the gain-line and not behind it. If it is necessary to clear the ball from the breakdown, then it must be done quickly. If the ball is stuck among bodies, it may have to be pulled out of the ruck.

Run

When arriving at a breakdown, the Scrum Half should approach with his head up and scan the options, looking for gaps around the

Continued on page 19

The Scrum Half spotted the gap before he had the ball.

A. DECISION MAKING AT THE BREAKDOWN

Activity	Key learning points

Pick and Go

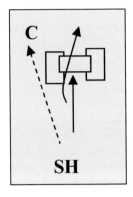

- SH passes ball to coach.
- Coach places ball in front of shield.
- SH runs, picks and goes.

Decision-making at the breakdown
- SH passes ball to coach.
- Coach places ball in front of shield.
- SH approaches the ball.
- There is a defender beside the ruck.
- If defender stays, SH passes.
- If defender moves away, SH can have a break around the fringes of that ruck.

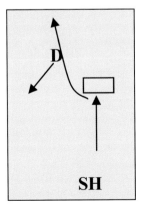

- SH adopts low body position.

- Step beyond the ball (lead with one leg and shoulder) as lifting the ball.

- Acceleration: short strides and keeping low.

- Ball in two hands.

- If hand-off necessary, move ball away from contact to far shoulder.

A. DECISION MAKING AT THE BREAKDOWN – (continued)

Activity	Key learning points

- As above but now encourage off-loading out of tackle.

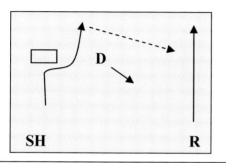

- Ball in two hands and push through and around tackler's back.

The reverse flip

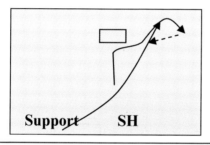

- Pass behind back.
- Keep hand up high.

Continued from page 17

edge of the ruck. There are times in a game when the opportunity to run is more likely to occur, usually from a quick, rucked ball after getting behind the defence. After several such rucks in a row there should be space, and the good Scrum Half will be aware of the potential to make a break.

Restart Kick Receipts

When receiving a restart kick from half-way, the Scrum Half will look to the options depending on where the ball lands. If it is a short kick on the locks, 9 will generally move the ball to the Fly Half and play; if it is a short kick infield, 9 will look to use the blind-side; following a long kick into the 22m, 9 will organize runners off the second phase or box kick.

Kicking

Tap Penalties

It is normally the Scrum Half's decision to take a tap penalty quickly to launch an attack before the defence has organized, and thus

Continued on page 22

Support players have made space for the Scrum Half to get the ball away by clearing out defenders.

Good body position, with shoulders square and hands pointing to receiver.

B. APPROACH TO BALL AND PASSING

Activity

Key learning points

Grid 10 x 10m. 2 lines of players in single file

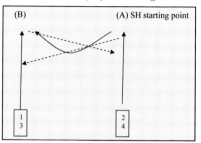

- SH passes to 1, who runs to end of grid (B), puts the ball through his legs. SH runs to (B) and passes to 2 who does the same as 1.
- Runners rejoin opposite line; SH keeps running and makes 10 passes before swapping with someone else.

- Low body position on arrival at the ball; it should be adopted early and maintained up to collection and distribution of the ball.
- The 'banana' approach brings the player front-on to ball
- Rhythm of pass is very important. Player should think of a 1-2-3 count to get appropriate momentum.

Grid 10 x 10m. 1 player in each corner. Each take turns as SH.

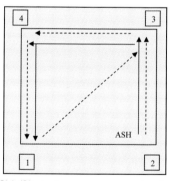

- Concentration is key at all times.

- Acting SH (2) starts sequence, passing to 3, who places ball.
- SH runs to collect and passes to 4 and then 1. Then he makes the diagonal pass to 3. He goes back to his starting position and 3 now starts the sequence (to 4, 1, 2, then diagonal to 4, then 4 goes).

Development:
Each pass is a pivot pass. Scrum Half approaches ball by running to centre of grid first. When picking up ball, his back should be to the receiver of the pass.

C. PULLING BALL AWAY FROM CONTACT AREA

Activity
Key learning points

Pulling the ball away from a breakdown with bodies in the way and defenders with hands over the top of the ruck (using tackle shields as the bodies).

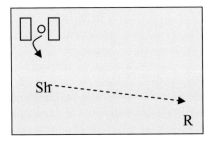

- Pull the ball out and up, towards the chest, before passing.

- Ensure a good grip.

- Ensure there is control of ball before attempting to pass.

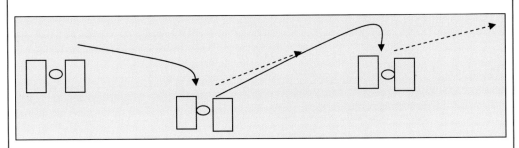

Execute a series of 3 passes away from a crowded breakdown (balls stuck between shields), then sprint back to start.

Continued from page 19

gather momentum in attack. The 9 should stay on the mark where the penalty was awarded. A team-mate should retrieve the ball, which may be in the possession of the opposition or have been thrown away by them. A quick tap kick might open up the opportunity for the 9 to run or move the ball to another runner. It is preferable that the Scrum Half does not take the ball into the tackle but instead uses one of the big forwards to do this.

Box Kick

The main kick available to the Scrum Half is the box kick from a scrum, ruck, maul or a driven ball from a lineout. The best position for this kick is from a scrum 10 to 15m in from the right-hand touch-line or from a driven lineout. The perfect kick will be parallel to the touch-line with enough distance and 'hang time' (the length of time the ball is in the air) for the Right Winger, who is giving chase, to arrive under the ball. It is essential to get the ball high for no more than about 25m long.

The Scrum Half has pulled the ball from the breakdown and taken a stride backwards to clear the debris.

Technical aspects: the Scrum Half stays low, left foot pointing at receiver, shoulders square to receiver, and follows through with the hands.

A. BOX KICK

Activity	Key learning points

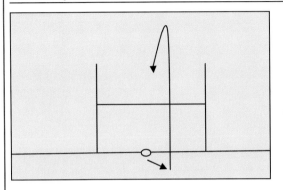

Activity

- Place ball under crossbar and on goal-line between the posts.
- Take step back and box kick ball over crossbar to land 15–20m downfield.

- SH box kicks to partner 15–20m away.
- See grouping as partner places ball on ground where he catches it.

- SH kicks either into the box or a grubber.
- The first player there either falls on the ball and pops it up to support players, who interpass.
- Or the first player goes beyond the ball, jumps and collects and passes.
- The ball might be tapped down so the support must not go lateral but must come from deep.

Key learning points

Feet position:
- As if passing to FH, reasonably wide base.
- Take just one step:
- Movement should be sideways and backwards.
- Common fault is to take more than one step.
- Other fault is to take step sideways but not backwards.

Placement of ball:
- Hold ball in palm of hand.
- Hold hand still and keep hold of ball for as long as possible.
- Hold ball at approx. 45-degree angle.
- Contact is made underneath the ball, sending it end-over-end 'backwards'.
- Common fault is for the hand to move away too early and to drop down.

Leg follow-through:
- Follow through as high as possible with a smooth action. Avoid 'stabbing' ball.
- Hold the ball higher to gain extra distance by producing a larger swing.
- Kick UP and THROUGH the ball

The head:
- Keep head down as long as possible.
- Common fault is for kicker to look for the ball too early so head comes up.
- Chest should finish facing towards the touch-line rather than facing forwards down the pitch. This is to avoid the kick travelling too far and flat.

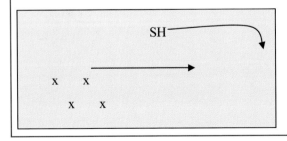

A. DEFENSIVE ROLE AND ORGANIZING THE DEFENCE AT PHASE PLAY

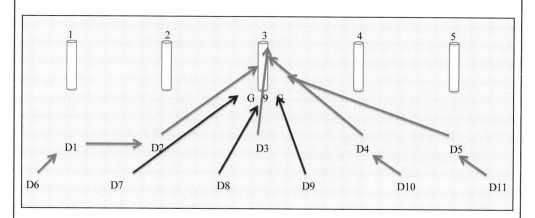

Activity

1 5 tackle tubes numbered off. Coach calls a number.
2 Nearest player (D3) tackles the tube.
3 First player (D4) goes for ball on feet.
4 Second (D2) and third (D5) players enter the ruck to block either side of first player.
5 Second wave of defenders come up to front line.
6 One player goes to guard on the right, another goes to guard on the left, one goes to 9 position
7 Remaining players align on back foot and go up man-for-man on to the remaining bags.

There must be a call for this kicking option, as it has to be chased if it is to be utilized.

Should the opposing winger retrieve the ball, pressure from the chaser may cause the ball to be dropped. If the ball is caught, then the catcher will be tackled and will have to release the ball or be tackled into touch. The kicking side thus retains the advantage and the Scrum Half has achieved a successful outcome!

Defensive Role

The personal defensive duties for the Scrum Half at the set piece depend upon field posi-

tion, and what type of set piece it is. The Scrum Half should ensure full communication with the back row and the Fly Half.

Own Restart

If the drop-out is a short kick, the Scrum Half will follow the ball because it may be quickly recycled. However, if it is a long kick, the 9 will hang back with one of the forwards (No. 8) and wait for a returned kick. If the return kick is a very good box kick, then the 9 should let the No. 8 take the ball. It is important for the big forwards to bear the brunt of the physical encounters, not the 9, who must remain in

A. DEFENSIVE ROLE AND ORGANIZING THE DEFENCE AT PHASE PLAY – (continued)

| Activity | Key learning points |

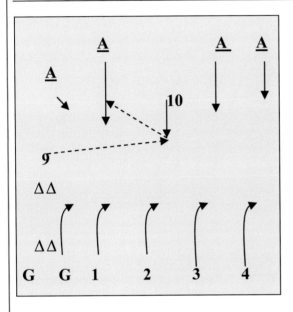

Description:

- 4 cones placed in square formation to identify last feet of a ruck.
- 9 and 10 run game-specific lines and deliver the ball to support players running inside, switch, and so on.
- Once defence makes tackle, tackler and closest defender go down on one knee with attacker to form ruck, setting the next offside lines.
- Coach delivers second ball to 9, counting from 5 to 1 so that both defence and attack can realign.
- Activity is repeated.

Key learning points

- Guards align either side of the ruck behind the hindmost feet.
- Defenders align on the inside shoulder of their opposite attacker, a half-step behind the defender inside them.
- When 9 touches the ball, defenders move forward off the line.
- Roles: guard takes pick and drive. If 9 runs, guard looks to take ball runner on inside of 9. If 9 delivers to 10, guard looks to take wide inside ball off 10 close to ruck.
- First defender takes 9 if he runs. If 9 delivers ball to 10, he takes inside runner off 10.
- Second defender defends against 10. Only when 10 delivers the ball outside do any of the inside defenders push to the ball.

- Development: attack uses different running lines to put pressure on defence.

the game to continue to be the link with the backs. However, if the kick is too long, the 9 should look to pass the ball and link with the Full Back to launch a counter-attack.

Own Drop-Out

If there is a short kick, the Scrum Half will follow the ball; if the kick is long, 9 and the hooker (No. 2) will cover in behind the

Pace and power through the defensive hole…

chasing line for a possible chip kick over them by the opposition.

Box Kicks

After executing a box kick, the Scrum Half will drop back to cover the wing position and any return kick the opposition may make,

thus creating the possibility of a counter-attack.

Lineouts

The Scrum Half stands at the front of the lineout and follows the ball in. The jumpers can thus see the 9 all the time; the Scrum Half

…with determination…

…and strength.

Protecting the ball.

The offload starting…

has full vision of the field and is giving no indication to the opposition about where the ball might be thrown. In open play the 9 plays a covering role behind the backs, following the ball across the field deeper than the first-up tacklers, to cut out any chip kick, tackle any attacker who might get through the front line defence, and then cover the wide break. The 9 should always be available as the last line of defence, if a cover tackle is required in the corner to save a try!

Scrums

From a scrum on the left of the field, the Scrum Half's role is to cover the opposition Fly Half or the first centre if the Fly Half switches with the 12. However, if playing against a less experienced No. 8 or Scrum Half, it may be better to pressurize at the base of the scrum to stop the movement at source. From a scrum on the right side, the Scrum Half's role is to put pressure on their 9, then hold the blind-side for a possible switch back blind. From a scrum in the midfield, the Scrum Half covers the right-hand channel close to the scrum, in case the ball is passed to a first receiver on that side. The Fly Half will mark the left-hand side of the scrum.

Line of Run

The line of run after the ball is away from the scrum depends on field position. For scrums on the left-hand side and centre, the Scrum Half will follow the ball. If the opposition have wheeled infield, the 9 will be tackling around the fringes of that scrum because it is likely the opposition's No. 8 will pick up and go. From scrums on the right-hand side, it depends what happens at the scrum: if the scrum stays square, the Scrum Half will harass the opposition Scrum Half, then follow the ball as it is passed to their Fly Half; if the scrum wheels infield (against the grain), because the opposition forwards have dominance, the Scrum Half will retire to the next most likely phase of play.

*...and successfully
completed.*

Phase Play

The organizing of the defence close to the breakdowns is the responsibility of the Scrum Half and it is very important that he should drive the forwards with constructive comments. If the ball is moved wide, the Scrum Half sweeps behind the front line of defence as a second line of defence.

The Scrum Half's defensive role is to tackle any player coming through the centre of the action. Communication is vital but not just from the Scrum Half – all players must talk, listen and react. The 9 should make sure that his side does not overcommit players to the breakdown lest the opposition have an advantage of numbers and is able to outflank. The Scrum Half directs his defending forwards after counting the numbers that the opposition has on either side of the breakdown, from the inside – in other words, starting with the defender nearest the breakdown and ending with the one who is farthest away from it. If there are fewer defenders than attackers the defending side should leave the farthest runner from the action unmarked, and get the cover or a drift defence to deal with him.

The opposition potential runners off the side of the ruck or maul have to be marked. To overcome the problem area at the edge of the breakdown, a guard (or post) is placed on the inside shoulder of the first defender. The guard does not mark anyone; he protects the inside shoulder channel not the fringes of the ruck. He covers any inside break or a runner coming on to an inside pass. The inside defender holds the inside channel and only goes when the ball does. The principles of who goes where are determined by the arrival times of the players. The defence should move up simultaneously at either side of the ruck, with defenders drifting across after the ball once it has passed them.

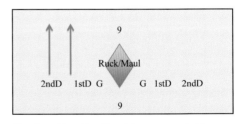

Guard on either side of breakdown to cover inside shoulder of 1st defender.

Development of Specialist Physical Skills

Training emphasis should be on the following:

- achieving good accelerative speed;
- keeping a low body position at speed;
- getting into fast running from all positions, for example, on the ground;
- agility – pace and direction change over short distances;
- fast repetitions with short recovery.

All sessions should include:

- warm-up (to include approx. 5 mins of continuous shuttle runs over 25m if in a group of four or more);
- basic running drills (such as high knees, back flicks, high skipping); and
- warm-down.

So a sample session might look like this:

1   Standing starts over 20m, varying starting position.
2   Varying 'lead' foot.
3   Both feet on the line.
4   Run with ball in both hands.
5   Shuttle runs over 20m, stooping to pick up and put down ball
6   Shuttle runs over 10m, but turning in the opposite direction (to left or right) each time.
7   Shuttle runs over 20m, stopping at each end for press-ups/sit-ups.
8   Starts from on knees, on back, facing wrong way, and so on.
9   Pace changes over 25m: for example, at 80 per cent then hard last 5, 10, 15, 20m.
10   Walk back recovery. Repeat exercise.
11   Direction changes at pace over short distance: for example, run for no less than 10m at an angle then straighten and sprint flat out for no less than 15m. (Vary angle and direction so that players take off from both feet.)

Agility Drills

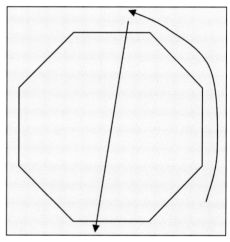

Circle formed by cones. No. 9 jogs around circle anti-clockwise and, on command of coach, sprints through the cones to the far side of the circle. Then starts jogging clockwise until the coach's command to sprint again to opposite side of the circle. The number of sprints and distance around the circle are varied. Development involves weaving in and out of cones: running forwards; running backwards; keeping back square to inside of the circle; keeping front square to inside of the circle.

ENDURANCE

The Scrum Half is working hard for up to six phases of play, so it is vital to develop endurance in training.

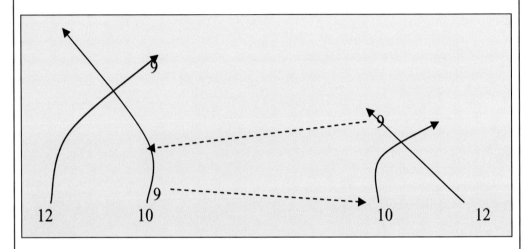

In the exercise, a 10m wide channel is set up, with two Fly Halfs, each with another runner outside him. The ball is passed from No. 9 to 10, who switches with 12. Tackle is called, the ball goes down inside the channel, and 9 passes to the second 10 with 12 outside him. The 9 supports this player, who, when tackled, puts the ball down; the 9 now has to pass to the first 10, who continues the sequence. This drill encourages the No. 9 to deliver passes of varying length from the ground from either hand. The Scrum Half is working hard for up to six phases of play, with appropriate work:rest ratios (varying between 1:2 and 1:5).

Endurance

In the exercise, a 10m wide channel is set up, with two Fly Halfs, each with another runner outside him. The ball is passed from No. 9 to 10, who switches with 12. Tackle is called, the ball goes down inside the channel, and 9 passes to the second 10 with 12 outside him. The 9 supports this player, who, when tackled, puts the ball down; the 9 now has to pass to the first 10, who continues the sequence. This drill encourages the No. 9 to deliver passes of varying length from the ground from either hand. The Scrum Half is working hard for up to six phases of play, with appropriate work:rest ratios (varying between 1:2 and 1:5).

SCRUM HALF: ENDURANCE DEVELOPMENT – GAME RELATED

Activity

Key learning points

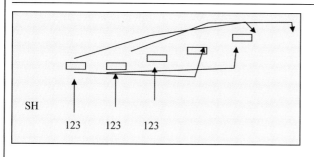

- Length and width of whole field. Start in one corner.
- 4–6 shield holders
- SH starts the drill by passing to first group; then acts as SH at every succeeding phase
- 3s. Ball carrier hits pad, goes to ground, 2 & 3 clean out.
- Groups rejoin line and Shield holders run to rejoin line of shields.

- Straighten line of run early.
- Hit with outside shoulder.

- Ball held in arm further from defender i.e. inside arm in this case.

- Curl in with empty arm

- Shields held low to encourage low cleaning out.

Development of Specialist Mental Skills

Leadership

'A leader is one who knows the way, goes the way and shows the way.' Anon

The most important mental and personal characteristics of the Scrum Half are the ability to communicate and organize, characteristics of leadership. A dearth of leaders on the field may be a result of authoritarian coaching, with players being told exactly what to do and when. Coaches need to be aware that players want to be respected and listened to and to feel that they have some say in what goes on. In order to develop as a decision-maker on the field, a player should be encouraged to be self-reliant, given the chance to lead, and empowered to create and implement his own game plan. A Scrum Half, in particular, should be involved in running the team. Many a Scrum Half makes a fine captain, often leading by example, and also being sufficiently articulate to talk to (and about) the team.

Communication Skills

In developing leadership skills, the Scrum Half needs to know what to say and a coach will have to help him with the content. The Scrum Half needs a good handle on game plans and tactical considerations. Too many coaches tell their Scrum Halfs to communicate, but do not explain what they should be communicating!

Reaching valid decisions is not easy for a player who is in the thick of the fray. In a time pressure situation, the Scrum Half is confronted with complex and rapidly changing perceptual displays, and information from the ball, support players and opponents, and it is in this context that he has to decide upon the most appropriate response. Knowing where and when to look are important skills. The coach must help players to decide which sources of information are relevant and which ones to ignore. Video-based techniques can help improve visual search in rugby – by stopping the video at specific times and requiring the player to specify what will result from the action, links can be drawn between cues and actions.

It is important to establish a meaningful relationship between the information extracted and subsequent behaviour. Coaches should therefore attempt to improve anticipation and tactical decision-making by teaching the Scrum Half to focus on relevant cues and by explaining their importance to performance.

A constant barrage of words from the Scrum Half will quickly lose effect – the forwards will soon stop listening! The 9 must choose the right time to speak and say what has to be said as succinctly as possible. When talking to the forward unit, a Scrum Half has to understand that there is a time to give information about what is required (at training, pre-game, at half-time, during the play at a ruck, or a set piece, and so on), but there is also a time to consider the emotional needs of the team and give inspiration.

CHAPTER 3

THE FLY HALF (10)

Checklist of Positional Skills and Attributes

Technical

- Ability to control and manage the ball under pressure even when in receipt of a poor pass from 9.
- Quick and accurate passing – short and long, off either hand and under pressure.
- Accurate and effective kicking off either foot: drop kick at restart and for goal; tactical kicking (bomb, grubber, chip, wiper); kicking from defensive situations (into touch, along tram-lines).

Tactical

- Good tactical sense (decision-making) to read the game. Ability to do the right thing at the right time.
- Decisive, calm, accurate and confident calling of moves.
- Understanding of gain- and tackle lines with the ability to play on the edge, bringing others into the game and through the tackle line
- Excellent understanding of the team's kicking strategy.
- Excellent communication skills.
- Capacity to threaten the opposition at all times by being unpredictable.
- Control of direction off phase ball.
- Ability to organize and control close-in defence and bring up centres on to the opposition midfield.

Physical

- High work rate and level of concentration, supporting own passes.
- Quickly getting into position for the next phase of play.
- Ability and speed to threaten blind-side defence.
- Elusive running skills: acceleration and agility to draw defenders and to penetrate when the opportunity arises.
- Physical defensive commitment: an effective tackler to stop powerful runners and maintain a high tackle rate.

Mental

- Confidence in calling options.
- Cool temperament under pressure.
- Perky/cheeky/adventurous.
- Quick action and reaction.
- Pro-active thinker but good capacity to react too.
- Good understanding of options.
- Awareness of own body language, which might reveal the planned move to the opposition.

The Specialist Role of the Fly Half

It may well be true that a good Fly Half is made in heaven and that the requisite skills, insight, reactions and decision-making for this position are instinctive. Even so, a coach can always help a good player to become a better

The defending Fly Half is being targeted by the bigger attacking forward.

one. The good Fly Half knows that, if he is to progress and develop his natural talents, there is no substitute for hard work. Skills have to be honed, a basic philosophy and understanding of the game have to be expanded, and speed of thought or reactions must be continually improved.

Like the Scrum Half, the Fly Half plays a pivotal role in the team in both attack and defence. Both players need to be sufficiently robust to cope with big forwards running at them. At the very least, the 10 must be a competent tackler. There are ways and means of protecting the 10 when the opposition have the ball, so that someone else – the Open-Side Flanker, for example – takes over his defensive responsibilities. Above all, what is required of a Fly Half is a thorough

understanding of the game. The 10 must understand the reason for passing or kicking or running, and must manage the 9 who, in turn, is managing the forwards. A good team will not function well with a weak Fly Half. The ideal 10 has to be a controller, varying his game, exploiting all options and keeping the opposition guessing.

Coaches often describe their Fly Half as either a 'kicking Fly Half', or a 'running Fly Half'. If a Fly Half is very dominant in one aspect of the game, however, he is of limited use because the opposition will be able to develop coping strategies. A kicking Fly Half with a dominant right foot, for example, will be nullified by a flanker approaching the 10's right side and forcing the player to kick with the weak left foot. It is vital for the Fly Half to practise the

A daunting sight! This Fly Half has cut down his own options by standing flat and close to the Scrum Half. His only option is a pass because he cannot accelerate due to lack of space, and he cannot kick because the defenders are too close.

A running Fly Half…

Or a kicking Fly Half?

whole range of kicks, from chip and grubber, drop-kick restarts, and cross-field, to spiral and end-over-end punts, and not solely off the strong foot. Work must be done on the weak foot as well.

A kick for territory – Fly Halfs require a wide range of skills.

The Fly Half takes up a position behind every phase of play, always in contact with the 9. The distance from the opposition at which the 10 stands depends on a number of factors. The 9's pass may be slow, giving the 10 little chance to escape the attentions of the opposition players who are racing up. In this case, extra time can be bought by standing further away from the defenders.

It may be that the 10's own ability to catch and give a pass is slow. Passing skills have to be mastered, and, once they have been, the confident 10 will be able to stand flatter, to interest defenders and give them less chance to react. The Fly Half will also need accelerative speed and good footwork to sprint through gaps and off-balance defenders.

Development of Specialist Technical and Tactical Skills

Tactical Decision-Making: Where and How to Attack

Scanning

The Fly Half must control the pattern of play, calling the shots from the set pieces and from phase plays. He is only over-ruled by the captain deciding on a change of strategy or by a player further out who believes there are opportunities there.

Even before 10 gets the ball in hand, the situation must be weighed up and the field scanned, so that the decision can be made whether to move the ball, run for space, take the ball into contact or kick. The Fly Half is bombarded by information coming from players outside and inside, and is at the same time scanning the fluid situation in front and weighing up where team-mates are in relation to the shape and numbers of the defence. It is vital that the Fly Half has the ability to filter all the cues – disposition of the opposition defence, quality of the possession, the field

TACTICAL DECISION-MAKING
– WHERE AND HOW TO ATTACK

Activity 1

Scrum Half fed a supply of balls.
A succession of players take the ball running and call out which side and how far out, for example, 'wide right' or 'close left'.

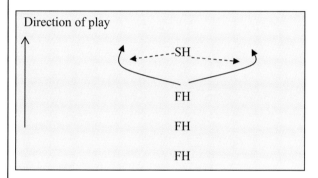

Progression: two lines of players.
- Coach calls '1 and 1'; two from the first line come out, to receive a pass from SH.

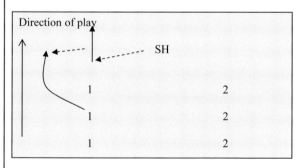

- First receiver passes to second nominated player.
- Coach can call '1 and 2'; '2 and 2'; '2 and 1'. The first player nominated receives the first pass; the other has to get outside to receive a pass.

Key learning points

- Verbal communication with SH is essential; SH is looking to his front most of the time and ball watching, so has no time to look back to find out where FH will be.

- At set pieces, SH has time to look at FH and visual communication may be used.

- Take a flat pass and cross the gain-line quickly, if there are no defenders in front.

- Step into the pass and get on a straight running line.

TACTICAL DECISION-MAKING – WHERE AND HOW TO ATTACK – (continued)

Activity 1	Key learning points

Progression: two defenders on either side of the contact area.

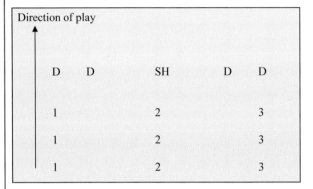

- Coach calls, for example, '1, 2, 3' or '1, 1, 1' or '2, 3, 1', and so on.
- First player nominated receives pass from SH, second nominated receives a pass from first nominated; third receives last pass.
- First player nominated shouts 'left' or 'right' to SH.
- First player passes to second before the gain-line; third must tell the new ball carrier where the supporting player – on the inside or outside.

- Verbal communication with SH is essential; SH is looking to his front most of the time and ball watching, so has no time to look back to find out where FH will be.
- At set pieces, SH has time to look at FH and visual communication may be used.
- Take a flat pass and cross the gain-line quickly, if there are no defenders in front.
- Step into the pass and get on a straight running line.
- Run on an arc to straighten line and fix defenders.
- Fix defender before making pass. Do not pass too early or too late.
- Passing too deep allows the first line of defence to drift on to outside men.
- If pressure is on ball carrier, pass; if pressure is on outside player, hold on and attack gap.

position, and relevant contextual elements (such as the weather, the time in the match, the current score) – and take the correct tactical decision with the minimum of inspection time. Often, a Fly Half will be seen looking at the breakdown, then looking around at the disposition of support players and then turning to look at the opposition before looking back at the breakdown. There is no need for this. If the Fly Half just looks at

the far posts from wherever he is on the field, the whole field to the front and side, including support players, the defenders, the contact area and the ball, will be in his field of vision. This gives more time to interpret what is happening and make a decision on which option to take.

Continued on page 45

TACTICAL DECISION-MAKING – WHERE AND HOW TO ATTACK – (continued)

Activity 2

Key learning points

Direction of play

```
                    D3
                    D2
                    D1
                    SH

    IC          FH          IC

    IC          FH          IC

    IC          FH          IC
```

- Defenders are lined up in 3s behind a ruck or maul. There is a Centre on either side of the Fly Half when approaching the contact area.

- Defenders step out into channels on either side of contact area on the coach's signal.

- FH reacts to defenders in deciding which direction to attack. He attacks the least-defended side – where there is only one defender or no defender.

- Centre on the far side, who is not immediately involved, must try to support and offer another passing option.

- Progression: a wing with each centre and 4 defenders.

- Once defenders have moved into initial defensive positions, and FH has decided which side to attack, the defenders are to cover back on the coach's signal.

- Head up, scan field and go to least-defended side.

- 'Where is the space?', 'Where are the gaps?', 'How much time do we have?'

- Mental arithmetic: 'Where do we outnumber the defenders?'

- Run on an arc to straighten. Force inside shoulder to point back towards the ball. Run square.

- Run at defender to fix him.

- The depth to which FH takes ball depends on whether there is space in front or a defender and how much time there is to fix the defender and get pass away.

TACTICAL DECISION-MAKING – WHERE AND HOW TO ATTACK – (continued)

Activity 3   Key learning points

- 5 v 5; Channel 20 by 20 metres; 3 Zones
- Defending backs are numbered off.
- Coach gives ball to attacking team and calls two numbers.
- The nominated backs of defending team run back, leaving a big hole or two holes in the defence. The attacking backs react and go through. (e.g. here the coach nominates 2 and 5 to retreat)

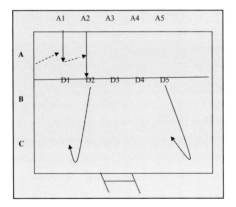

- If space is wide out, Fly Half will pass early so centres can get away their passes, but not so early and so deep that the defenders can just drift across and fill in the hole.

- If the gap is close in, fly half will take ball flatter and hold on to ball a little longer.

- What matters is the passing line in relation to the tackle line.

Progression:
- Call out one number so that there are fewer options.
- Disguise the calls (mix up the numbers) so that, where the gaps are, does not become predictable and the attack is forced to scan properly.
- once through gap, ball carrier must go for player/s who has/have dropped out.
- That defender is active.

Progression:
- The coach can manufacture movement by jogging forwards or backwards before distributing the ball to the attacking back-line
- He can give the ball to the attackers when retreating and under greater pressure from defence

TACTICAL DECISION-MAKING – WHERE AND HOW TO ATTACK
– (continued)

Activity 4	Key learning points

One ball and 5 cones.
22 metre grid.

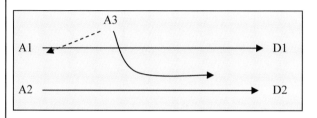

- A3 passes to A1.

- Players A1 and A2 with the ball attack the defenders D1 and D2

- As soon as Players A1 and A2 have crossed the halfway line, Player A3 joins the attack.

- Cyclic – Players A3 and A1 become defenders D1 and D2 and A 2 goes to A3. D1 and D2 become A1 and A2

Developments:

- Second Defender can be more active by coming in on BSW or staying on Second Attacker. Fly Half has to decide which passing option to choose.

- One SH with ball joins 3 attackers through a tunnel to take on 3 defenders. Attacking line now join the queue at the defending end. Defending line jog through and join the queue at the attacking end

Key learning points:

- A1 to fix D1 – do not pass too early or D1 will drift

- A3 come into line off A1's shoulder

- If D2 jams in, A1 passes to A2

- If D2 stays on A2, A1 passes to A3

- A3 times his run

TACTICAL DECISION-MAKING – WHERE AND HOW TO ATTACK – (continued)

Activity 5

- Two sets of backs. The coach wanders around the playing area with the ball, sometimes forwards and backwards.
- The Scrum Half of each team stays with him.
- Everyone repositions in relation to the ball.
- The coach releases the ball to attacking Scrum Half who passes to the Fly Half who has to read the defence.

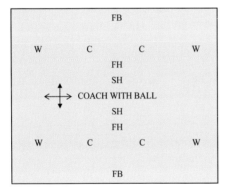

Progression:
- If there is a breakdown, the coach shouts "Tackle"
- The attackers all have to head for the coach who has now secured the ball at the breakdown.
- As the attackers home in towards him, the coach gives the ball to the other unit who counter-attack.

Key learning points

- Count the numbers.

- See the space.

- Fix defenders by running at them at pace.

- Aim at inside shoulder of defender to fix him.

- Do not pass so late that next man cannot get his pass away.

- If you feel the pressure on you, make the pass; if you feel the pressure on the outside man, hold onto the ball and dummy.

Continued from page 40

Kicking

The Options

The options for the Fly Half from phase play depend on numbers in attack against numbers in defence, the shape of the defence, where space is available and the line speed of the approaching defenders. To clarify: there might be the same number of attackers as defenders but, if the width of the defensive line is narrow compared with the width of the attacking line, then the space is out wide. In that case, the Fly Half will transfer the ball quickly to that area.

The opposite is also true: if the defence is spread out so that there is space between defenders, the correct option is to put a runner through the defence. The Fly Half might read this situation as an opportunity to attack by using runners off the inside or outside shoulder; also if the Fly Half believes that there are no attacking opportunities wide out; that defenders need to be sucked in and another phase set up with the intention of breaking up the defensive organization.

One other option might be to change direction. This would be appropriate where there is a phase play in the middle of the field. The Fly Half knows that by coming back against the grain – in other words, against the direction of the original attack – there is an opportunity to create mismatches by launching backs against slower front-five players who are defending that side.

If the ball being delivered is slow and defenders have a chance to reorganize their front-line defence, and all defenders are up and in that defensive line, space may be visible behind it. The option then is a tactical kick (chip or grubber) with chasers to re-gather the ball. The Fly Half then has to be aware of the sweepers in the second line of defence – normally the opposing Scrum Half, No. 8 and Blind-Side Wing – and where they are.

Importance of a Kicking Strategy

It is important to have a kicking strategy because it is the easiest way of gaining territory and the most efficient way of finding open spaces when well-organized defences are keeping line breaks to a minimum. Weather conditions may dictate that, on the day, the kicking game is probably a wiser strategy than the passing game; it is a 'safety first' option. Kicking also provides variety to the game plan and can keep the opposition guessing. If the only way the opposition can score is through the use of the boot, kicking long can keep the opposition out of range of point-scoring via penalties or drop goals.

Clearance Kicks

When his team is in its own 22 and under pressure from a set piece or retrieving an opposition kick, the Fly Half will be keen to get the ball off the pitch and preferably 'into the stand', to reduce the opposition option of taking a quick throw. If the ball is passed back into the 22m zone, it cannot be kicked directly to touch. The clearance kick then is down the 15m channel, looking for maximum distance and space, keeping the ball in play. A chasing strategy should be planned. Normally, three players (often the wing, the Inside Centre and the Open-Side) should chase, to put pressure on the receiver and force errors. A second line across the field is made up of the players not involved in the chase and not involved in the third line. It is the job of the second line to work together to prevent the counter-attack if the first line fails in its task of retrieving the ball. The kicker, Full Back and No. 8 tend to make up the third line, ready to receive the return kick and launch their own counter.

For the technique for successfully completing such a kick (spiral punt or end-over-end punt), see Chapter 6, 'The Full Back'.

Territory-Gaining Kicks

From a central position either the Scrum Half or Fly Half can kick to the corners, with a low trajectory but with the intention of keeping the ball in play. This forces the opposition to kick or run back. If the ball does go into touch, the intention is to pressurize the opposition lineout on their own line.

Re-Gain Kicks

A re-gain kick is intended to gain territory and maintain possession and it must be chased. A number of kicks fall into this category: the Scrum Half box kick; the Fly Half's bomb ('up and under'), which is the high kick on the Full Back, with chasers and sweepers underneath it to contest for a 50-50 ball; the cross-field kick to the unmarked wing; and the chip or grubber just behind the opposition midfield, with the centres running on to the ball.

In order to execute a chip kick successfully, the kicker should scan for space beyond the approaching defenders. A poor chip kick will cause a perfect attacking opportunity for the opposition against limited defenders. Control of the ball is crucial as the Fly Half will be running at pace when attempting to execute the kick. The ball should be released from two hands, and not thrown up or pushed down. The head should be down and over the ball on contact and the Fly Half should avoid looking at oncoming defenders. Striking the ball lower to the ground than when spiral or end-over-end kicking creates more control while kicking on the run. The Fly Half should look to aim to catch the ball himself, by judging the pace at which he is going and the target space area.

The drop goal: the ball is angled slightly back; a longer final step generates power; the non-kicking foot points to the target.

Drop Kick: Drop Goals

Teams will have a drop-goal routine play, where the aim is to work towards the middle of the pitch and in range of goal for the Fly Half. There are a number of key factors for executing the drop goal:

- The ball is held away from the body to allow a longer final step, which in turn generates more power from the back lift of the kicking leg.
- The toes of the kicking foot point away.
- The ball is angled slightly back.
- The hands hold the sides of the ball with one hand slightly back.
- The kicker aims to make contact early as the action is to go through the ball, for distance.
- The ball hits the ground and bounces up before the strike.
- The foot hits the ball just below its centre.
- The non-kicking foot points to the target.
- Shoulders are square and the weight goes forward.
- The follow-through is important: the direction of flight is determined by the shoulders being square and the position of the front foot.
- The kicker should look once at the posts, then concentrate on visualizing them, as there will probably be no time in a match situation to look again.
- The ball should be taken on the kicking foot side of the body, as valuable time will be wasted if readjustment is needed. (Practice with the Scrum Half is important for time-saving precision.)
- The ball is taken in the hands, not the body (for the same reason).

The drop goal. The ball is angled slightly back, a longer step generates power and the non-kicking foot points to the target.

● The kicker's position will be affected by where the ball is coming from. If the ball is won on the left side of the pitch, the kicker should stand to the right, so that the leg swing is protected from inside defenders (for example, 7). If, however, the ball is won on the right, the kicker needs to stand a bit deeper to reduce the angle and build in protection from inside defenders.

Programme to Practise Drop Kicking At Goal

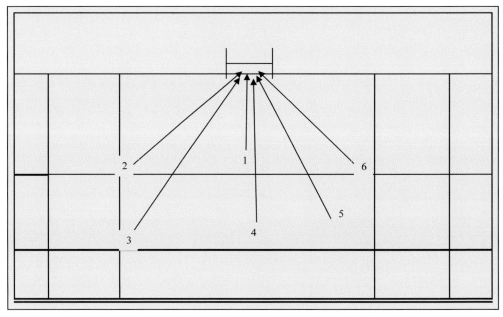

Take kicks from each of the above positions. The quantity in the following table is flexible

POS	QTY	date	date	date	date	date	date	date	date
1	10								
2	5								
3	3								
4	5								
5	3								
6	3								
TOT	29								

Drop Kick – Restarts and 22 Drop-Outs

The aim of this important kick is to re-gain possession through chasers. The tactic may also involve a long kick downfield, forcing the opposition to counter from a distance. Chasers will hunt them down and the break-down, hopefully, will be some distance from their own goal-line. The short-kick restart, with as much 'hang time' as possible, is the usual requirement to allow chasers to get to the ball and re-gain possession.

There are a number of key factors to consider when executing the drop-out:

- The ball, which is angled slightly back, needs to be held not too far from the body.
- The hands hold the sides of the ball, with one hand slightly back.
- The ball is released by moving the hands to the side, neither throwing the ball up nor pushing it down.
- Head and shoulders remain square to the intended target area.
- The body goes over the ball, so that the kicker is leaning slightly forwards.
- The non-kicking leg bends as the ball hits

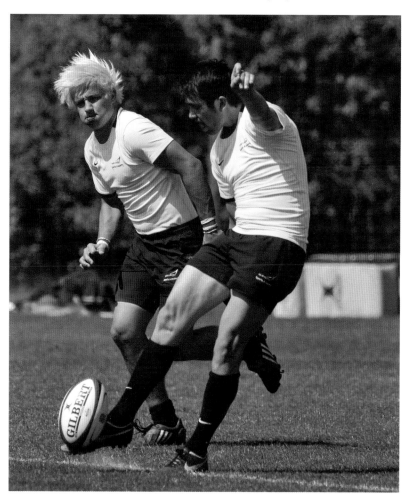

Executing the drop kick – there are a number of key factors to observe.

the ground, which allows the ball to be struck on the foot's upward curve.

- The toes of the kicking foot come back slightly towards the leg; they are not extended.
- The kick is slightly delayed, as the aim is to strike more up than forwards.
- Striking the ball on the half-volley with the ground will lead to a lack of height, but more distance.

- The kicker should aim to come right under the ball, striking up and continuing the foot upwards after contact for increased height.
- The head must be kept down – lifting the head will cause mistiming of the strike – with the eyes focusing on the ball and on the point of contact.

DROP KICKING – RESTARTS: PRACTICES

Practice 1:
- Stand as close as possible to the posts.
- Work at regularly getting the ball over the crossbar from the minimum distance possible.
- Get the feel of lifting the ball into a quick elevation.
- Feel a soft leg swing rather than a kicking action.

What is the distance and how long is the hang time (the time ball is in the air)?
Measure the distance in a direct line from the centre spot to a standard kick-off landing area, about twenty two strides. Ask the best chaser to run the distance as fast as possible and time the effort. With this time and having paced-out twenty two steps, it is possible to calculate hang time and distance.

- Kicker behind the posts and measure out the distance just calculated to a point straight ahead, which will be on the 22. Mark a box with cones about 2x2 metres in size.
- Then measure 5m back from the goal line and place a cone at that point.
- Kicker to kick the ball over the crossbar to land the ball in the coned area.
- Once the kicker is comfortable in being able to kick the ball over the crossbar, move forward about a metre towards the try line, making it harder to get the ball over the bar. Concentrate initially on getting the ball up and over the bar.

Practice 2: Full kick to target on 10m line
Move to centre field to practice sessions with the forwards chasing the ball. For 22m restarts, alter kicking distance to what the team/chasers require. A successful restart strategy is at the worst a 50/50 ball winning opportunity. If your kick is right and placed to the best chasers, you will have a far better than 50/50 chance of regaining possession; the better the kick and the chase become, the greater the chance of your team's success.

Programme to Practise Drop Kicking – Restarts

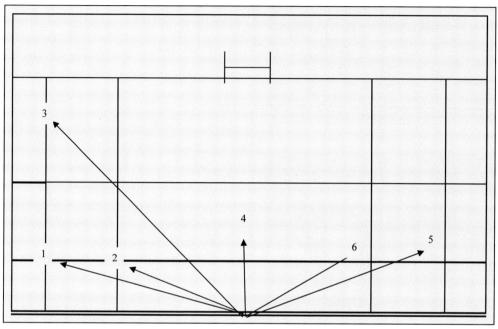

Use cones as targets to and hit the distance regularly.
Take kicks to each of the above positions. The quantity in the following table is flexible.

		date	date	date	date	date	date	date	date
POS	QTY								
1	5								
2	5								
3	3								
4	5								
5	5								
6	5								
TOT	30								

Constant practice is necessary to achieve consistency.

Development of Specialist Physical Skills

Speed

Fly Halfs operate in a limited amount of space and need to have the capacity to accelerate past the gain-line and through a gap in the defence. During the pre-season, the Fly Half should be working on developing a fast top speed. As the in-season approaches, the sprint distances should decrease. By the start of the in-season, sessions should concentrate on acceleration. Training should include sprints involving a change of speed and direction, as well as reaction drills.

Acceleration Sprints

Speed is gradually increased in training, from a rolling start, to jogging, to striding out, then maximal pace with a maintained quality of running style. This is designed to improve acceleration, which is important in the game, particularly in defence and support.

A training session might proceed as follows: jog try-line to 22m; sprint to half-way line; slow down to 22m; jog to the try-line; walk back full length; do a set of 3–6 runs × 2. Alternatively, the session might proceed as follows: accelerate 10–20m; jog for 50m; accelerate 10–20m; jog for 50m; walk for 100m; do a set of 3–6 runs × 2.

Hollow Sprints

Perform two sprints with a recovery period in the form of light running. This form of exercise mirrors the changing pace of the game during one sequence of play.

1 Accelerate for 10m, jog for 30m, accelerate again for 10m, then walk for 100m × 4; undertake 3 sets.
2 Accelerate for 20m, jog for 40m, accelerate again for 20m, then walk for 120m × 4; undertake 3 sets

Mix the two sets together, for example, 1, then 2, then 1; or 2, then 1, then 2.

Change Gear Sprints

Gradually increase from rolling start to jogging, to striding out to 75 per cent pace, to maximum, as if 'changing gear' every 20m, up to 100m. Walk back recovery for 100m.

Speed Endurance

The Fly Half has to remain alert and focused throughout the game and good levels of endurance are required so decision-making is not affected by fatigue. The 10 has an enormous amount of chasing, cover and support running to do, so, between repetitive sprints, a quick recovery has to take place. Aerobic endurance enables the player to carry out sub-maximal work for an extended period of time, keeping him running through the game.

Aerobic endurance is best achieved by relating the intensity of training to heart rate. To train aerobically, the pulse rate needs to be raised to between 65 and 85 per cent of maximum heart rate. At any higher than this, the body is not being trained aerobically. To work out maximum heart rate, the formula of '220 minus age' is used. A 30-year-old's

Speed Endurance Game-Related Exercise

Player organization:
- 5 balls spaced out in a line.
- Scrum Half with Fly Half.
- 9 runs to each ball and passes to 10.
- Repeat off other hand.

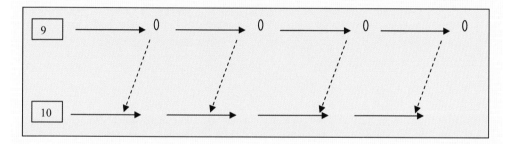

Progression 1:
- Number each ball.
- Coach calls which ball to be played next.
- This involves some retreating and readjustment of alignment.

Progression 2:
- Fly Half communication: decides where he wants the ball passed and shouts 'wide left/right' or 'short left/right', and so on.

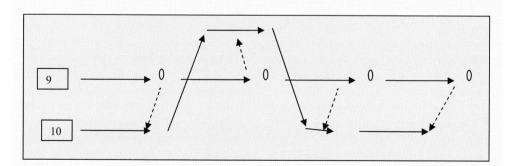

maximum heart rate is therefore 190 beats per minute. The ideal training range for someone of this age is 65 to 85 per cent of maximum heart rate, that is to say, 123 to 161 beats per minute.

To be fit for rugby, training should be undertaken three to four times a week with the sessions lasting at least 30 to 40 minutes. Most of the player's aerobic endurance should be built up in the foundation period of training, June to mid-August, when longer sessions, lasting 45–60 minutes, are best. In season, this amount of training would leave players tired for games, so it should be reduced to two or three times a week.

An aerobic training session can consist of continuous low-intensity activity. Running must be included, as this is what players do in a game, but the repeated impact of constant running can cause injuries to develop, particularly in the 'big fellas'. One alternative is interval or 'fartlek' training, which involves intermittent increases in pace as the player feels like it, followed by lower-intensity work until he feels ready to increase the pace slightly again. Walk/jog/sprint/jog/walk pyramids are undertaken, but moving continuously, aiming to increase the time spent jogging and sprinting and to decrease the walking time.

Development of Specialist Mental Skills

Decision-Making

The Fly Half is one of the most important tactical decision-makers on the field. While it can be argued that the coach has largely taken away the need to make so many tactical decisions because game plans are a series of sequenced moves, the Fly Half is still bombarded by verbal and visual cues, which can have a detrimental impact on his decision-making. Examples of these cues are the shouted messages arriving from team-mates. Coaches can also give mixed messages by setting planned sequences and then telling everyone to go out and 'play what you see in front of you'. If a gap appears in the defence, does the Fly Half exploit it or stick to the pre-planned sequence?

What is decision-making and how can it be improved? There are two different types of decision-making. The first is analytical, when a strategic type of decision is made at half-time or during breaks in play, when the captain decides a change in game plan because of the way the match is evolving. It is rational and calculating. It might also lead to the Fly Half calling a move or sequence of moves while a lineout or scrum is forming. The other type of decision-making is intuitive and reactive, when there is no time to think. This might be the case when, for example, a Fly Half has planned a particular move, but sees the opposite defender slip, and decides instinctively to run into the space that has been created.

Discussing situations and options with the coach will help the Fly Half to improve his analytical decision-making. The questioning approach is very much in vogue among coaches these days. By asking the right questions, it is possible to contribute to the learning process by taking the players out of their comfort zone. Using this approach alongside visual recordings of matches, the player's tactical understanding is expanded and decision-making improved.

The Fly Half's intuitive decision-making will be improved through experience. It is possible to help the player to understand what to look for in order to respond to cues more accurately. However, the more often the player personally experiences various situations, the better. By adopting a 'game sense' approach, with small-sided games leading up to fully opposed sessions, the coach can guide

Player Awareness

Organization:

- All players in a large grid. Run in any direction. Avoid contact.
- Utilize space: run into gaps; avoid crowded spaces.
- Plenty of balls. Pass to anyone. Pass may go in any direction.

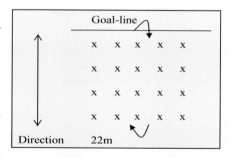

Activities:

- 'Ball down': ball carrier puts ball down and picks up another.
- 'Change': exchange the ball with someone else.
- 'Throw': throw the ball over someone's head and run around to catch.
- **One ball between two**. Each pair keeps passing: short passes/long passes/any type of pass, such as one-handed, around back, overhead, and so on.
- 'Down': put ball down; partner drops on ball, pops it up or gets up quickly.
- Roll ball, pick and run, roll ball, etc.
- Roll ball, fall on it, get up, roll ball, etc.
- High ball, get under and catch.
- **Groups of 35 players** working together but moving about the grid all the time: 1 puts ball down, 2 falls and secures it, 3 steps over and lifts it to 1, etc. 1 throws ball in air, 2 goes up to collect and distribute to 3 or tap it to 3, etc. 1 throws ball over head, 2 catches, steps into 1 who has now turned and defends. 3 helps 2.

Relevance:

- Development of peripheral vision.
- Warm-up of body and mind. 'Switching on', to get players thinking.
- Ball skills, hand/eye co-ordination and assessing which type of pass is applicable.
- Develop the concept of using space.

Traffic Passing

Organization:

- In groups of 4 passing a ball and jogging over distance of 22m.
- Continuous running and passing for a specified time between the goal-line and 22-m line
- When the line gets to the 22-m line, it is to turn and run back to the goal-line. Other waves will be coming through and leaving the start line at regular intervals. Avoid contact.
- Keep the distance between each wave.

Relevance:

- Improve peripheral vision. Players should focus their eyes exclusively on the ball (passing and reception) and use peripheral vision to locate and to avoid other players.
- Warm up the mind.

Extensions:

- Execute a loop somewhere in the line, or switches, or long, miss passes followed by inside pass.

the players to self-discovery by continually questioning them: 'What were you trying to do when…?', 'How might you have … in order to …?', 'What else could you have done to …?', 'How might you have …?', 'What would have been a better option to take, and why?', 'What other options were available to you and what might have happened had you taken another option?' This questioning approach, in match-simulated situations, will improve both the self-awareness of the player and his intuitive decision-making ability.

Peripheral Vision

Great players stand out because they are able to demonstrate their skills at a high level under pressure, as well as seemingly having plenty of time in which to perform them. This capacity is associated with the player's mental attributes, an ability to read the play effectively and to react appropriately to the situation. A player's capability to read play depends on a number of factors. One of the most important of these is anticipation, which depends on the efficient processing of information relating to events around them in order to choose the right action.

Put simply, players receive the majority of messages or cues through what they see. One player's vision may be the same as another's, but his experience and training will determine his ability to detect and interpret some cues earlier than others. In addition to the normal vision used in day-to-day living, a player's peripheral vision is most useful in rugby. Developing an awareness of what is seen 'out of the corner of the eye' can be incorporated into training exercises and players trained to use this peripheral vision could become more competent at performing basic game plays. If a player is deemed to have 'taken his eye off the ball', he has probably not been trained to use peripheral vision and has attempted to use eye contact to perform the task.

There are a number of drills that can help players become aware of and train the use of their vision. These drills can also benefit players' concentration skills.

CHAPTER 4

THE CENTRES (12 AND 13)

Checklist of Positional Skills and Attributes – Inside Centre

Technical

- Good distribution skills with the ability to execute a variety of passes accurately under pressure over a variety of ranges, from short push to long spin passes, to bring the forwards into play.
- Ability to commit defence with good lines – straight runner to keep attack alignment.
- Good contact skills for ball retention with ability to stay up in tackle.
- Off-loading skills in and through the tackle
- Very strong, aggressive front-on tackler on either shoulder, to step up and knock back defence.
- Ability to execute a range of kicks, both in attack and defence: cross-field kick or wiper (long diagonal) in attack; long punt when playing for territorial advantage; grubber or chip kick to put himself or a runner through into space and/or behind a flat defence.

Tactical

- Key decision-maker and communicator, especially in defence and attack from broken play.
- Playmaker with vision and decision-making qualities.
- Unity in defence and attack with 10 and 13.
- Axis for much of the back-line attack, getting play moving forwards towards the gain-line.
- Communicator and organizer of defence of 10, 12 and 13 in particular.

Physical

- Explosive speed and power to pressurize defence line – straight runner.

Fixing defenders: the pass is made when the body weight is on the back foot (the foot further from the receiver), taking care not to transfer the weight from the back foot to the front foot (foot nearer receiver). Timing is crucial too – can the next player get a pass away?

Fix defenders by aiming at inside shoulders.
(Continued overleaf)

Strong straight running by this Centre and the defender shapes up to take the tackle, feet knees bent, straight back, shoulders square.

- Size and strength, direct and capable of attacking the gain-line close, controlling the contact, developing phase play and committing defenders to the tackle.
- Accelerative speed through small gaps, in limited space.
- High work rate – key support role at tackle when appropriate.

Mental
- Courage – a strong tackler who is prepared to stop his opposite number or any supporting forwards head on.
- Determination in tackling and work rate, with the ability to back up and speed to re-form.
- Leadership qualities and good communication skills, to act as the link between the half-backs (9 and 10) and the outside backs (13 and wing). Ability to relay calls that have been made by the half-backs and to get feedback from the outside backs on the defensive line-up of the opposition, so that the appropriate moves can be called.

Checklist of Positional Skills and Attributes – Outside Centre
Technical
- Quick and accurate passer off either hand, with ability to execute long, short, float and miss passes, to put his Full Back and wings in the clear.
- Ability to stay up in tackle and to off-load at or through tackle.
- Two-handed ball carriage, for continuity and distribution.
- Ability to commit defence with running lines, and promote support players, inside and out.
- Kicking skills especially chip and grubber, in behind opposition backs, and long kick out of defence.
- Aggressive tackler, to create turnover opportunities and break up attacks.

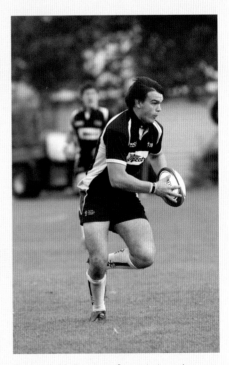

Two-handed ball carriage, for continuity and distribution. (Continued opposite)

Tactical

- Good organizer, with an understanding of attack and defence.
- Ability to read the game and apply good tactical sense.
- Playmaker with the pace and vision to create the outside break and release support players.
- Key decision-maker, especially on defence and when attacking from broken play.
- Good alignment and cohesion with inside player (12) on all facets of attack and defence.
- An organizer who can read defensive situations, marshal the defence, and shut down the opposition back line.

Physical

- Good linear pace to make the outside break.
- Explosive speed and power, with the ability to step off either foot and beat defenders on inside or outside.
- Agility to get into space and use it effectively.
- High work rate as a key support player at tackle and following kicks and cover defence.
- The strength to take the ball up to the opposition and set up continuity play.

Mental

- Good communication skills.
- A hard mind to stop attackers in the area.
- High work rate.
- Speed in action and reaction.

The Specialist Roles of the Centres

Selection is not an exact science. Each of the centre positions – 12 (the Inside or First Centre) and 13 (the Outside or Second Centre) – demands certain skills and attributes in isolation, but when selecting team players it is more important to consider how each will complement the other. The game plan is a major factor in the selection of the ideal centre pairing. If the strategy is to attack the wide channels and to play an expansive game, the major prerequisite of the Inside Centre is an ability to pass quickly and accurately to the Outside Centre. If, however, the game plan is to keep the ball close to the forwards, the main quality required would be physicality rather than handling ability. The player would need to be big and powerful and able to break tackles, off-load in the tackle and retain possession. If a team has two players of similar ability, there can be an element of mix and match. Collectively, the two positions are vital in implementing the crucial task of crossing the gain-line so that the forwards are going forwards. The centres also need to create space for their wingers, the potential try-scorers.

Another consideration in selection is whether an Inside Centre complements the Fly Half. For example, if it is possible to put together a left- and right-footed pairing, that may be a luxury that increases a team's options.

There are a number of attributes that are needed in both centre positions: a good understanding of the principles of attack and defence; good peripheral vision, to see space where the attack should be focused, and to see where the numbers game is in their favour; the ability to take decisions based on the defensive line-up, position on the field and quality of possession; the ability and courage to make head-on shoulder tackles against players who are trying to run through them, or to make side-on arm tackles against players who are trying to run around them; the ability to off-load to allow continuity; good contact skills to retain possession of the ball; good running lines as either ball receiver or decoy runner; and a good understanding of the role as first, second, third, fourth player to arrive at secondary phases and employ appropriate ruck or maul techniques.

There are also certain attributes that are specific to each position. They are two different positions and perform two different roles at centre. With more space available, 13 tends to be the more attacking runner, with extra pace and agility. The Inside Centre works better in confined spaces, tends to be more physical, and a strong runner with the vision and distribution skills to be a playmaker. Many centres at the top level of the game would have the attributes of a 12 and a 13.

The biggest difference in the two positions is in the space available, with the inside player enjoying the least of it. The focus here now is on a general assessment of what we expect of a player in each of these specialist positions.

Development of Specialist Technical and Tactical Skills

Passing and Running Lines

Fixing Defenders by Straight Running

Although the first direction of the Fly Half should be forward, the weight on the Scrum Half pass can be such that the Fly Half has to run slightly across field to take the sting out of it. The whole threequarter line will be running towards the touch-line unless the Inside

In defence: the centre will align on the inside of his opposite number. The starting position is with inside foot forward. The first step will be off the inside foot driving outwards and approaching the attacker from the inside. If attacking, the outside foot is forward so the first step is back towards the ball.

This centre is shaping to pass long. His weight is shifting to the front foot, he is running sideways and his immediate defender will now drift onto the receiver because he is in no danger of being side stepped and beaten on his inside; he has not been fixed.

Centre angles back and straightens the line. To prevent this, the starting position for the Inside Centre is with the outside leg (the one further from the ball) forward. When the centre starts running, the drive off the outside foot will be back towards the ball and the line will be straightened. This preserves the space on the outside, fixes the defenders and prevents the defenders from drifting.

Keeping the running lines straight preserves space and makes support easier. The keys are as follows:

- The centre's shoulders are towards the ball source.
- The running line is picked up before he gets the ball.
- The centre starts by running at the defender (inside hip?) rather than away from him.

Creating Space

The focus for the both the Fly Half and Inside Centre is on fixing the defending inside players and putting the ball either short or long, depending on the support runner's call. The ball carrier will endeavour to create or widen a space for the support carrier to run through. The supporting player needs to pick a good angle, with the options being wide or short. Players often make the mistake of simply running straight at a space. All this does is allow the defence to adjust and tackle the player with an easy side-on tackle. The change of angle must be left till late. Changing the point of attack by changing the angle through the ball carrier and support player creates space effectively.

The success of this play requires excellent

Continued on page 65

Fixing a defender by aiming at the inside shoulder.

FIXING DEFENDERS

Activity

Key learning points

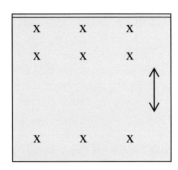

- In 3s, I ball.
- Relay – lateral passes to end player – ball passed on to next line who come out to meet.

Development:

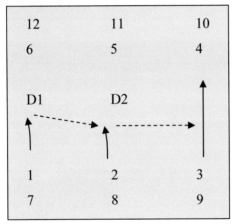

- Add 2 defenders:
- I fixes D1 and passes to 2;
- 2 fixes D2 and passes to overlap 3;
- 3 runs on and hands on to 4.

- 456 do same – NB D1 and D2 have to move across channel and turn around to face 4 and 5 (overlap is 6); they must do the same when ball is handed on to 7.

The catch:
- Stretch hands towards passer but not straight (or too long in getting pass away).
- Catch to be made at the line of the shoulder, just outside hip.

The pass:
- Use wrist action and forearms instead of long arm swing action.
- Short, sharp, snappy, powerful.
- Ball to be released just off far hip.
- Chest square on to defenders.
- Pass when body weight is on back foot (foot further from receiver).
- Do not transfer weight from back foot to front foot (foot nearer receiver).
- Timing of passes – can the next player get a pass away?

The run:
- Fix defenders by aiming at inside shoulders

ATTACKING GAPS BY CHANGING ANGLES/GOING THROUGH THE DEFENCE

Activity

The short ball

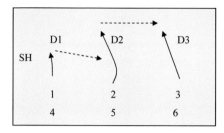

- SH with a supply of balls to feed each line.
- Static defenders.
- 1 fixes D1 and passes to 2.
- 2 aims at outside shoulder and calls short.
- 2 breaks through and passes to 3.
- 3 must accelerate through to support the breakthrough.
- 456 do the same and the subsequent lines.

Development 1: the wide (fade) ball:

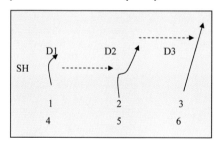

Development 2: the diamond

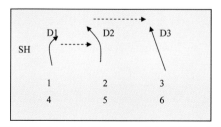

Key learning points

'Unders' pass:
- Both 1 and 2 aim at outside shoulder of respective defenders and switch to inside shoulder.
- Weight of pass – aim to far shoulder of receiver.
- Look for 'cues' to pass. When the defender's head, shoulders, feet turn away from the support player and towards the ball carrier or attacker, he is likely to be committed.
- Ball carrier staying on feet after passing to stay alive as a support player.

'Overs' pass:
- Both 1 and 2 aim at inside shoulder of respective defenders and switch to outside shoulder.
- Weight of pass – aim to far shoulder of receiver.

The Diamond
- 1st receiver attacks inside shoulder then moves to outside shoulder of defender.
- 2nd receiver attacks outside shoulder and moves on to inside shoulder of defender to receive short pass.
- 1st receiver blocks out any movement by 1st defender to cover inside shoulder of 2nd defender.

MOVING DEFENDERS

Activity

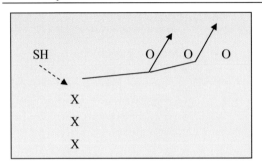

- 3 shield holders.
- Rest lined up to the side.
- SH feeds a ball.
- First receiver runs laterally across the face of the 3 static defenders.
- Side-step through first or second gap.

Key learning points

- Strong side-step.
- Look as if to pass to a runner on outside.
- Move ball to far arm so closest defender cannot get to it.
- Fend off inside defender when going through gap (in this case, it is the one on the left).

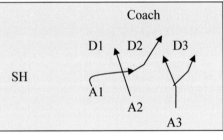

- Centres provide FH with options.

Progression:
- Add 2 attackers to first receiver.
- First receiver runs across the face of the defence.
- Second receiver provides option of a switch.
- Third attacker chooses either to take a short pass or a wide pass.

Progression:
- Coach stands behind middle defender and steps into one of the spaces between defenders as attack develops.
- Attackers have to decide which space to attack by reacting to which space the coach has occupied

Continued from page 61

passing skill, well-timed running and passing, good running lines of both players, good decision-making as to when to change angle, and good communication between passer and receiver. The 'Under' and 'Over' plays are simple, basic plays on which the foundations of line-breaking attack are built.

Passing

Passing has to be off both hands and must be accurate. If the receiver has to check and slow down due to a poor pass, the opportunity to penetrate or go round the defence has disappeared. The margins are that fine.

Supporting the Line Break

Once the defending line is breached, the ball carrier should be looking around for someone

Note weight on back foot, hand placement on ball poised to give a spin pass.

to make a pass to. It will not be long before he is confronted by cross cover defenders. Once the player is through, the options are to fix the cover defence and get the pass away

3 v 2: ball carrier steps in to attack inside shoulder of first defender; second defender steps in to take ball carrier or cover second attacking player, leaving third attacker free. If the ball carrier holds on and delays the pass, the support player will get tackled on receipt of the ball; the option is to miss out the support player and pass straight to the third attacker. The real option is to pass now to the support player, who has time to fix the second defender and get the pass away to the overlap, the third attacker.

or for the ball carrier and support players to change angles and make it difficult for the defence to defend in an organized way.

There should be immediate support available to the ball carrier. The attacking players should aim to flood the area behind the defensive front line with support by aiming at a spot 10m in front of them and trying to get to it as quickly as possible. They should then be surging through in numbers and ready to help.

Hand-Off or Fend

A centre should practise running with the ball at pace and beating opponents by change of pace, change of direction, breaking a tackle, dummy, side-step and swerve. In the centre, players rarely have the chance to beat their opposite numbers from distance, like a winger, because there is never enough time available; most of the time, the centre tends to be under pressure immediately from a tackler. Most breaks are not simply 1 v 1; the norm is

---

Skill development: Supporting the line break

- SH with supply of balls.
- Attacking threequarters lined up in 3s only 3m from 3 defenders. A 4th attacking player lines up on a cone 15m away (the Wing).
- Front-line defenders remain passive and do not move.
- SH starts the exercise by passing to 1 who passes to 2 on an unders line bursting through the gap.
- Real injection of pace comes with the 3rd attacker.
- Once through the gap a 4th and 5th defender lined up on cones behind the defensive line now join in the defence as the cross cover.
- Attack must score (3v2)

Key learning points

- A3 and A4 provide immediate support of ball carrier.

- A2, A3 and A4 should not remain on the same running line but try to move defence around.

- Attackers should communicate their positions to the ball carrier.

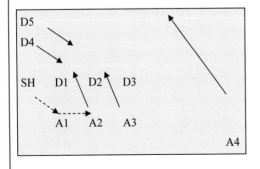

Line break! A perfect running style while carrying the ball in two hands, ready for the fix and pass or off-load in the tackle.

Expecting contact, this ball carrier has shifted the ball to the far arm and is preparing to hand off the incoming tackler.

more likely to involve the use of decoy runners, which can lead to a misunderstanding in the defence. The attackers will soon learn to recognize the signs of a confused defence.

The 'hand-off' or 'fend' is part of a player's evasive armoury, often developed by instinct. The use of a flat hand on the head of a tackler coming in low, or on the chest of a tackler coming in high, and a strong extended arm to keep the body and the ball away from close contact, is an effective evasive skill. The player needs to be able to transfer the ball into the arm furthest away from the tackler just prior to the fend-off, and spin. This means always keeping the body between the ball and the opponent.

The fend: ball moved to arm further away from contact, hand on tackler's chest.

Skill development: The fend	Key learning points
<ul><li>In pairs. One holds the ball in one arm and leans against partner, hand on chest as if fending off. Change arms.</li><li>Develop to fours. One pair in front with the ball and the other pair behind in support. Jogging pace.</li><li>First pair keep passing the ball.</li><li>On whistle player without ball has to make a low tackle on partner.</li><li>Ball carrier fends off.</li><li>Next pair take over, either having to pick up the ball or receiving a pass from the ball carrier.</li><li>Continue the movement.</li></ul>	<ul><li>Bent elbow.</li><li>Hand on shoulder/head/chest of tackler.</li><li>Open palm.</li><li>Push away</li><li>Ball in outside arm</li></ul>
<ul><li>3 shield holders.</li><li>Rest lined up with a ball each – in front of the 3.</li><li>Run at central defender and side-step either way.</li></ul> 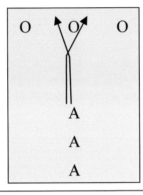	<ul><li>Strong side-step.</li><li>Move ball to far arm.</li><li>Fend off middle defender when going through gap.</li></ul>

Skill development: Side-step and/or fend

Key learning points

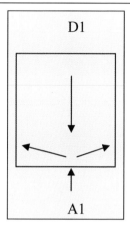

- Strong side-step.

- Good acceleration – stay low for initial few strides.

- Body language indicates an attempt to run one way; when defender falls for it, go in the other direction.

- On whistle, A1 picks up ball 2–3m inside the grid.
- A1 must score on one of the side-lines.
- D1 must try to stop A1 starting 5–6m away.

Kicking

The Wiper (Inside Centre)

Kicking is a necessary skill for this position. If the Fly Half is predominantly right-footed, options for an exit strategy from his own 22-m area can be devised if one of the centres has a good left boot (or vice versa). If the Outside Half wants a clearance or territory-gaining kick from a diagonal kick, it is better done from the Inside Centre position. If the Fly Half is under great pressure from the defending Open-Side Flanker, the advantage of having someone else in the line who can kick is obvious. Another kicker also brings a variation to the game plan, keeping the opposition guessing.

The aim of the wiper kick is to reduce hang time on the ball, which diminishes the chance of a defender fielding the ball before it hits the ground. This kick will be a spiral punt rather than an end-over-end punt, which tends to be in the air longer. The shoulders should be over the ball, to give it a low trajectory. The kicker should be selecting a target before getting the ball and should be working all the time with the Fly Half and other centre. His cues come from the position of the opposition Full Back and Open-Side Wing. If the wing is deep, the wiper should probably be cancelled, as it could be easily retrieved by that defending winger.

The kicker should aim not to kick too far because this would allow the defence too much time and space to retrieve the kick, and extra length also makes the chase harder for the kicker's team. If there is no left-footed kicker and a player has to perform a right-footed kick to the left touch, the kicker should align deeper in the 12 channel. In this situation, the kicking Inside Centre has a particularly important role. The extra depth is required because the ball will be closer to a

SKILL DEVELOPMENT: THE WIPER

Key learning points

- FH does not run too far, if at all.

- There are 2 pivots in 9/10 and 10/12 passes, both to be fairly static.

- 10 and 13 have the role of 12's eyes for an attempted charge-down by the defence.

- Must be an effective chase.

- The kick should stay in play so that the opposition have to kick it out.

- SH to feed 10 from simulated scrum, or ruck/maul.
- 10 pass to 12 to kick along the diagonal behind defending 11.
- 14 to chase and put pressure on 11's retrieval of ball.
- Development:
- An opponent acts as a flanker and moves towards FH from the simulated scrum or ruck/maul when SH's hand touches the ball.
- Involve more opponents and also supporting players who are to follow the kicks and try to re-gain possession.

- There must be an organized defence from the initial chase in case the opposition counter-attack

- Players should be moved around so that the best performers of the required skills are in the key places at the right time.

charge-down than it would be when performed left-footed to the left touch.

Tactical Kicks (Fly Half, Inside Centre or Outside Centre)
If the defence is difficult to break through – if the speed of approach of the defensive line is such that the midfield players find little room in which to operate – one of the major ways of getting the ball behind the advancing defence is the chip kick or high kick to the corner, or the grubber kick.

It is more difficult to pick up a rolling ball than to catch one in the air, so the grubber

The tactical chip to the corner is an effective attacking weapon, causing panic in the defence.

A one-handed off-load is an essential contact skill.

Activity: Kick to score

Kick to break down defence.

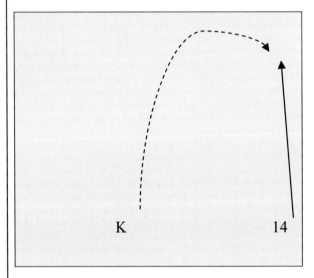

K   14

- K to chip kick the diagonal behind defending 11.
- 14 to chase, collect and score.

Development:
- Use the grubber kick.
- K to decide which kick to use.
- K to move wider to execute the longer, diagonal chip kick to the corner

Key learning points

Chip Kick:
- Release ball from two hands, without throwing ball up.
- Head is down and over ball on contact, trying to avoid looking at oncoming defenders.
- Striking the ball lower to the ground than when spiral or end-over-end kicking creates more control
- End-over-end kick:
- Communication between winger and centre that defence is narrow and the kick is a good option.
- Support runner (14) comes from out to in, so sight of the ball is never lost.

Grubber:
- Hold ball with seam parallel to ground with one hand on either side.
- End of ball points away.
- As it falls close to the ground kick just under the end of the ball so that it travels end over end.
- Let the ball drop until it is very low to the ground.

can be a dangerous tactical kick. The player retrieving the ball will also find that his peripheral vision is more limited. With his head down and eyes fixed on the ball, he is able to collect less information about the speed of approach and the proximity of the chasing attackers.

Such kicks can create uncertainty in the defence and make defenders rather more hesitant about their line speed. They may hold off on coming up too quickly, or the Full Back may hold back to cover the kick rather than joining the defensive line. This hesitancy creates space for the attacking line to keep the ball in hand.

The opportunity for the diagonal high kick to the corner for the wing can be created by a couple of secondary phases to pull the

A. CONTACT SKILLS IN DEFENCE

Activity: Role of the inside shoulder defender

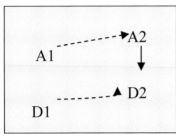

Groups of 4
Defender 2 on knees, Defender 1 on inside shoulder.

Attacker 1 passes ball to Attacker 2 who takes tackle, goes to ground and presents ball.

Defender 1 straddles ball and lifts it from low powerful stance.

Attacker 1 comes in to hit defender who fights to control.

Development
As above except no Attacker 1 – becomes Defender. 3. After turnover Defender 3 calls for pop to hit hole for deeper pop so pass ball away from contact area.

Development
Defender 1 steals ball, picks and goes – Defender 3 in support

Key learning points

- Protect inside shoulder of player opposite the ball carrier, by being behind by half-metre.

If the tackle ends up on floor,
- get nose over tackle and improve the condition of the ball for own team: turn over or slow ball down.
- Toe, knee, shoulder.
- Drop centre of gravity.
- To lift ball – arm inside leading knee for protection.
- Remove ball to safety point – farthest arm.

If ball carrier is on feet,
- pump then assist getting ball carrier to ground while looking to work on ball to get a turn over.
- Step over and pass ball.
- If second into tackle hit the upper part of body and either wrap ball or hit upper body and work to steal ball.

---

defence forward. Kicking in the opposition 22-m zone is an option, if the chances of recovering the ball are good and the defence is so efficient that it is impossible to score by running the ball.

Contact Skills in Defence and Attack

The Inside Centre must be physically strong. It is often very difficult or inadvisable to get the ball passed wide, so many game plans revolve around the Inside Centre taking the ball into contact, being a target for the forwards and creating a secondary phase by retaining possession of the ball. However, the main aim should be to break through the defensive line, and the centres should be

Continued on page 76

Activity: Counter-attack from tackle

Key learning points

A1 passes to A2. A2 runs into upright tackler D2, who works on the shoulders to open up the ball to be stolen before putting ball carrier to the ground. Try to put ball carrier on back so ball accessible for the rip. D2 in to help D1 steal the ball.

- Hit, wrap, rip.
- Squeeze ball carrier's elbows, then ball comes away.
- Come from inside shoulder of tackler.
- Tackle high with furthest shoulder.

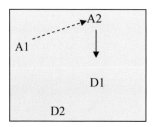

Development

Set up as above. Tackler on haunches hits ball carrier but not enough to knock off feet.
D2 comes in and focuses on ball carrier working to wrap up ball, or to hit, wrap then steal ball.
Tackle must come from side – ball carrier must stand strong.

Counter-Attack

7 v 4 or 5 v 3.
2 of the initial defending side are on their knees.
The attacking side take the tackle.
The player on the inside shoulder of the tackler steps over to win the ball and plays it away.
The new attack tries to get behind the new defence.

- Move ball away from turn-over point.
- Scan defence and attack either mis-match or get ball to free players on outside.
- Turn over – change mindset, get some depth, scan, talk, react.
- Attack with pace.

O	O	O	O		
1	2	3	4		
x	x	x	x	x	x
	k		k		

Player 2, 3 or 4 takes ball up into either player on knees for turnover / counter attack to start

B. OFFENSIVE TACKLING

ACTIVITY: THE DOMINANT TACKLE IN TECHNICAL TERMS

Key learning points

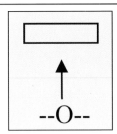

1v1 Tackler has arms behind back and drives into tackle shield with correct foot position from 2m.

Progress from walking to jogging – introduce three small steps whilst the shoulder is in contact with the shield.

Exercise 2
Same set-up but ball carrier wears body armour.
Tackler walks towards ball carrier who is holding ball behind back.
Execute tackle and knock the ball to ground.
Progress to ball carrier changing angle so tackler has to alternate tackling.
Practise sequence of the tackle:
- Foot position.
- Body position with hips square.
- Shoulder contact.
- Drive.
- Hands and arms grip tightly.

Development:
Ball carrier now holds ball in front of body.

Foot positioning:
- Shorten steps near target.
- Feet close in – strong base.
- Same leg, same shoulder.

Body positioning:
- Focus on chest hitting pad.
- Defend with eyes and feet.
- Head up, eyes open, chin off chest.
- Neck in extension position.
- Knees bent, body upright, sink at the hips.
- Hips square.
- Eyes focus on the target area for shoulder.
- Head close to the side of target.
- Head close, shoulders will follow close.
- Drive through the tackle with three small steps to keep the feet on the ground.
- Head in line with spine.
- Hands up in front of body as if boxing.
- Arms and hands shoot forward quickly on contact with shoulder.
- Strong grip, squeeze arms.

Leg lift:
- Head and leg lift on same side.
- Hook leg at base of the hamstring, just above knee to off-balance attacker.
- Target shoulder just below ball.
- Drive feet through the tackle.
- Put attacker on to back.
- Follow through to land on ball carrier.

Another one-handed off-load.

The tackling posture of the player in black – head down, back rounded (in flexion) in the lumbar and thoracic areas – will increase the possibility of a serious neck twist and flexion injury. If he were to bend at the knees, straighten his back, drive from his legs and hips, then lift his head and drive hard into the tackle, it would be a safer and far stronger contact, driving the ball carrier backwards.

Continued from page 73

looking at running through gaps rather than running at defenders. They should also be skilled in ball retention and the off-load. The other centre should be looking at how best to support the breakthrough and be ready and on hand to secure possession of the ball.

When not taking the ball into contact, the 12's role is to defend by tackling opponents head on. Both centres must, however, work together in defence and not in isolation. Working as a unit, with the inside player leading, the alignment should be the same as in attack. Constant communication is the key. The aim should be to shut down opposition space as quickly as possible, to make lots of tackles and hit hard. The first player makes the tackle, the second player attempts to secure the ball. Developments include wrapping the ball up if the attacker is standing, or pinching the ball if the tackle is made and the ball is on the floor.

C. CONTACT SKILLS IN ATTACK

Activity: Breaking the contact line, continuity

Key learning points

Exercise 1:

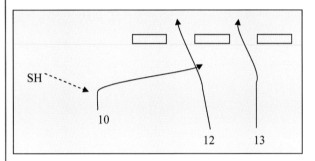

- 3 shield holders. SH feeds a ball to FH.
- FH runs across face of defenders and switches with 12.
- 12 busts the shields and passes to support runner, 13, who has accelerated through the defensive line.

Developments:
- Hit shield, spin through and off-load.
- Hit shield, with 13 in and grab ball.
- Add tackler behind shields.

Exercise 2:
- 10 and 12 dummy switch and 10 pops to 13 (or switches).
- 13 busts the shields and passes inside to support runner, 12, who has accelerated through the defensive line.

12 and 13
- Strong step, change angle late.
- Hold ball securely in two hands on chest.
- Drive low through tackle.
- Accelerate through tackle.

Fly Half
- Look as if to pass to a runner on outside.
- Carry ball in two hands.

Development of Specialist Physical Skills

Whilst strength and conditioning regimes concentrate on aerobic, anaerobic, strength and power training, conditioning the body to cope with the impacts that are such a major part of rugby is often ignored. Because of the frequency and the extent of the contact involved in carrying the ball or tackling, centres are more susceptible to injury. It is crucial that they use the proper biomechanics in the tackle and develop body hardness. Injury is also more likely to happen to a player

Activity 1

Several defenders with shields or wearing body armour spread 3m apart. A cone is placed 5m in front of each.

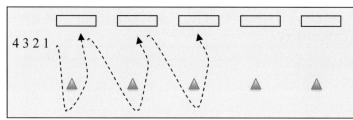

1   Player No. 1 goes around cone 1 and drives into the first opponent. The opponent comes forward towards the working player when rounding the cone.
2   No. 1 backtracks to cone 2, always facing the opposition. Player No. 2 rounds cone 1, and together on 2's call, they both drive into the opponent facing each of them.
3   They both backtrack to the next cone, facing the opposition.
4   Player No. 3 rounds cone 1 and all three, on 3's call, drive into the opponent facing them. They backtrack; player No. 4 rounds cone 1, etc.
5   When the attackers have worked against all six opponents they take over positions in the defensive line.

Activity 2

Several defenders with shields or wearing body armour, each holding a ball, are spread 3m apart. A line of tackle bags is placed opposite them (10m away), and a line of cones between them. The working players are grouped at the start line.

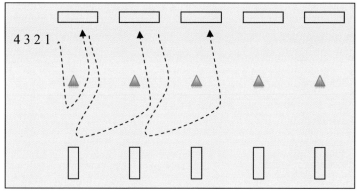

1   Player 1 rounds the centre cone 1, drives into the first opponent, clamping the ball and driving opponent backwards 2–3 paces (simulating a wrap-up tackle). The opponent comes forward towards player 1 on rounding the cone. Player 1 releases the opponent, turns, goes face down on the ground at the cone, then makes a driving tackle on bag 1, recovers and moves to the next centre cone.
2   Player 2 rounds cone 1, and together 1 and 2 take on opponents 1 and 2, turn, hit the ground, tackle bags 1 and 2, and go to the next centre cone to wait for player 3
3   Player 3 starts the sequence on rounding cone 1, and so on (players 4, 5, 6). In order to work together the attackers take their timing from the inside player, the attacker at position one.

who has the least momentum on entering the contact situation, so centres must be offensive defenders as opposed to waiting for the offensive player to make contact.

Good contact conditioning, together with power conditioning throughout the season, will help to reduce injury and make a centre more effective in both attack and defence. However, contact conditioning does not mean simply letting players knock over tackle bags, and run into players holding shields and falling to the ground. Poor body mechanics in contact can be confirmed. Sports-specific training in contact conditioning should provide players with proper tackling technique, which converts the power and explosiveness and strength qualities generated in the gym into real on-field efficacy.

Development of Specialist Mental Skills

Courage: 'What lies behind us and what lies before us are tiny matters compared to what lies within us.' Anon

The centres are heavily involved in the game, both in attack and defence. The nature of their positions means that they have to be physically strong and also brave. Theirs is not a contact but a collision sport. Players are running at them and they are running at players at pace, to break or make head-on tackles. To do this match after match, it is vital to develop mental as well as physical resilience.

Mental toughness means different things to different people, so it is best considered as an umbrella term for a number of different psychological attributes.

Perhaps the mentally tough performers are those who train hard, play hard, perform consistently well under pressure, stay focused even when injured, and make the necessary

sacrifices in the drive to success. It is clear that mental toughness is made up of different aspects of psychological behaviour, and it is up to the coach and player to decide what attitude should be displayed in a match in reaction to various scenarios, such as losing, being behind in a match, being in a winning position, suffering a disputed referee's decision, making mistakes or struggling with form, playing against opposition who are very strong or, conversely, a team whom everyone expects to beat easily. In other words, it boils down to preparation.

In order to improve mental toughness, a number of psychological skills are needed and should be rehearsed until they become a habit. These might include maintaining a positive attitude when under pressure, composure after mistakes or bad refereeing decisions, or task focus when outcome expectations are high. These habits or behaviours can be coached and continually developed, using a number of well-known methods, including goal-setting, self-talk and imagery. A mental toughness programme can be as simple as a set routine designed to get a player ready physically and mentally before a game, and when returning to the field after half-time. This routine could involve going over the key tasks that will need to be performed on the field, both in the mind (for example, using imagery and self-talk) and physically (in training).

Mental toughness is an acquired skill. It comes to those who work hard on their preparation. In young players of potential, who do not have years of experience behind them, durability, resilience, consistency, discipline and toughness can be identified in a background check. For example, how many games has the player missed and why? Is the player organized and committed in other areas of life, such as education, social life, and other areas of interest?

One way of developing the discipline that is so much a part of mental toughness is to keep a daily diary. It is a challenge to go through a routine. If the player cannot perform the relatively small tasks of filling out a diary, setting targets, and correcting errors that the diary makes evident, it is doubtful whether he will be able to follow a full season's instruction or come through tough game situations. More elite players may not need to fill out a diary, because they will have the necessary discipline from years of hard preparation already. However, the young recruit should not be allowed to escape. If he is not committed to doing the little things and cannot complete all the disciplines through the week, there may be a fundamental problem, and his ability to perform consistently under pressure must be in question. The discipline to carry out the tasks that are required of him, even if they are seemingly insignificant, is the foundation of a player's future in Rugby Union.

CHAPTER 5

THE WINGS (11 AND 14)

Checklist of Positional Skills and Attributes

Technical

- Ability to beat opponents 1 v 1.
- Speed.
- Physical strength and power.
- Change of pace.
- Mastery of swerve, side-step and hand-off.
- Ability to perform chip and chase while running at pace, or grubber kick.
- Effectiveness in kick chase in sub-unit.
- Ability to deliver quick ball in contact and stay up in the tackle when required.
- Secure handling at pace.
- Accurate, long infield passing – up to 15–20m – from a static position.
- Ability to retrieve and field a variety of kicks under pressure.
- Box-kick defence.
- Catch and clear; fall and recover; catch and support.
- Rolling ball.
- Ability to jump and catch the ball in the air, both chasing and receiving kicks.
- Ability to kick effectively off preferred foot and, if required, off weaker foot.
- Ability to kick along the tram-lines (15-m channels) and chase.
- Ability to kick the high ball and chase and catch.
- Catching and positioning for cross-field kicks in attack and defence.
- Effective individual tackling technique, whether with space or tight.

Tactical

- Understanding of the role of the Outside Centre and Full Back and capacity to work with them for effective defence from open side.
- Ability to assess the need to enter a ruck or maul to win ball, or to stay out and defend wider or provide an attacking option.
- Understanding of back-three pendulum defence.
- Recognition of when to counter-attack and when to kick or pass on blind side.
- Understanding of blind-side defence to organize others effectively to defend from ruck, maul or scrum.
- Understanding of own defensive role from lineout, knowing where to stand and what to do when the ball has been either won or lost.
- Understanding of role in attack from open or blind side as ball receiver, decoy or link player.
- Ability to work with back division to create space in attack for himself or others by using good running lines and timing.
- Recognition of his own impending isolation and potential loss of possession, and ability to avoid this.
- Capacity to play either on the left or the right.
- Ability to pose a constant threat to the opposition by: changing starting position to pull opponents out of their defensive position; varying running line and point of

(Continued overleaf)

attack; being aware of blind-side options and entry from blind side as an attacking or decoy option; taking men on the outside, if there is space (to stretch the defence), or on the inside if close to touch (to keep the ball in play); really going for it when in sight of the try-line.

- Ability to read a game and to do more than just stay on the wing.
- Awareness, to keep the ball alive in 5-m channel, switching back off the touch-line.
- Full understanding of counter-attack.
- Total cohesion with Full Back and other wing.
- Good tactical kicking awareness.
- Effective team defence technique, particularly in back-three unit.
- Understanding of how to preserve space, pull defenders in and then swerve to beat the defender.
- Ability to fix defender and pass accurately to support runners.
- Understanding of and ability to execute tackle options, for example, the smother.
- Understanding of defensive positioning when defending a wide diagonal kick.
- Effective positioning and appropriate catching technique when defending a box kick.

Physical

- Pure pace to finish attacking opportunities and to close down players quickly in defence (linear speed).
- The ability to change direction, while at top pace, to beat defenders (evasive speed).
- Ability to move quickly from walking, jogging and sub-maximal speed to top pace, injecting a change of pace in reaction to changes in play.
- General full body strength for ball retention, tackling, contact skills and power development.

- Evasive footwork to avoid contact.
- Speed endurance – the ability to produce top or near top speed on repeated sprints, with short recovery for effective cover defence, and to finish opportunities even when fatigued.
- Accelerative speed – the ability to accelerate to top speed quickly from a number of starting positions, including getting up off the deck, standing still, and so on.
- Ability to maintain a high work rate.
- Initiative off the ball to create attacking opportunities.
- Willingness to chase and pressurize opposition whenever possible.
- Desire to get involved in the game at every opportunity.

Mental

- Spatial awareness – a good understanding of the position of players to recognize the most effective role in attack and defence.
- Ruthless edge to finish off attacking movements – determination and courage, particularly in contact situations, where there may be a need to fight to retain the ball and in chasing kicks.
- Focus and distraction control – ability to stay focused even when not directly involved in play, and a desire or hunger to work hard off the ball in order to get involved.
- Composure under pressure, avoiding panic and not rushing into decisions.
- Effective communication skills to liaise with a fragmented back-three unit.
- Confidence to play as first receiver – the more phases of play there are, the more likely it is that the wing will be the first receiver – and the confidence to back himself in attack
- Effective decision-making, with focus only on the relevant stimuli, both aural and visual.

The Specialist Roles of the Wings

Wings are chosen for their attacking ability, for finishing off passing movements and scoring tries. The wing is often alone when receiving the ball in attack, on his own against the rest. It is vital that a wing is a creator as well as finisher. The best will try to equip themselves with every trick in the book. Strength is important, to break tackles, hand off opponents and retain possession. Often the wing gets the ball where there are few defenders, and it is important to take out the tackler and make a pass to a support runner. Speed, change of pace, fend, bump, in and away, kicking, determination and courage are all prerequisites for good wing play. A wing needs to be an exciting runner who can counter-attack from an opposition kick and quickly re-gain ground.

If the opportunity for counter-attack is not available, wings should be able to kick for distance. They are instrumental in the kick and chase, as a retriever, a returner, and the first line of defence. The wings' work rate should be high as they work in tandem with the Full Back in defence. They also have a lot of running to do in attack, either with the ball or chasing kicks. With the long kick now a part of every team's strategy, the Full Back alone cannot cover the wide spaces at the back, and the wings must help.

When a coach is organizing a team, the players assigned to the wings are often those who are very fast, but have poor distribution skills, and might be a liability in the centre! However, this attitude will not develop those players, and the game has evolved to a stage where efficient core skills are required from all positions. The wings have, therefore, to be adept at catching and distribution just like any other threequarter.

It is not simply in attack where the wingers must perform. The defensive requirements are more demanding and just as important. Defensively, from the scrum and lineout, the Open-Side Wing has options on which position to take up. By standing wide and deep, he can cover an opposition diagonal kick. Once the ball has gone through the hands of the attacking Fly Half, however, the wing's priority will be to join the first line of defence by moving forward. If employing a 'rush' or 'blitz' defence, the Open-Side Wing will stand flat with his centres. If the attack goes open, it is essential for the defending Blind-Side Wing to cover across the field as a sweeper behind the front-line defence. Any opposition player breaking through the front-line defence should be targeted by the Blind-Side Wing.

A left-footed wing might do better on the left for kicking ahead, and vice versa. Similarly, it is difficult for a right-footed wing to step inside the cross cover if he is playing on the left. Whatever foot is the strongest, that is the wing to play on for kicking, side-stepping, and so on. The kicking foot is protected from the approaching tackler and any clearance kicks might be less likely to drift into touch.

The ball should be carried in the arm closest to touch – for example, in the left arm on the left wing – leaving the inside (right) arm free to hand off an approaching defender. The same applies on the right, where the left arm should be free. It is particularly important to hold the ball correctly to be in a position to hand off tacklers, or to off-load the ball by passing inside to any team-mates who are supporting. In defence, the Right Wing will line up inside the ball carrier and tackle with the outside shoulder – in other words, his strong side.

The ability to take kicks cleanly is crucial. If a player is deemed to be poor under the high ball then he will be bombarded by the opposition half backs all match. The most

Scoring tries – the main attacking role of the winger.

common situation in which a wing must field the ball is the long diagonal kick from the opposition Fly Half looking for touch. The defending wing should attempt to catch the ball on the full. If it bounces, there is the risk of losing control of the ball, as well as giving extra time for the opposition backs to come up to apply pressure.

Once the ball has been safely caught, the decision has to be made as to whether there is enough time to kick for touch (if within the 22), or if it is safer to hold on to the ball and wait for support. If the ball is caught outside the 22, it makes for a tricky dilemma: is it best to pass back to the Full Back inside the 22, kick the ball back long and aim for territorial possession, or attempt to run the ball out of trouble?

There are two golden rules to wing play:

1 The wing should keep himself in play at all times.
2 No matter who the outside player is when the opposing team attacks, that player must not be allowed to score.

Development of Specialist Technical and Tactical Skills

Evasion: Beating Opponents 1 v 1

A degree of pace is essential but some of the most effective wings are not necessarily the quickest. The key thing is to pose an attacking threat. If speed is lacking, the skill of breaking tackles becomes more important. Other than the well-known methods of beating a defender, such as the side-step, swerve or hand-off, wings have to develop the skill of

Go for it, but change the ball-carrying arm!

kicking into space while sprinting (the chip) and work on the grubber or push kick through a gap. The ball does not need to travel far but all attacking options are left open when the right weight is put on the kick.

An assessment of some of the following criteria will influence the wing's decision-making:

A strong side-step but the ball is held in the wrong arm. This player is not able to execute a hand-off with his right hand.

- Shall I run around the defender on the outside? Do I have the pace? Is there room on the outside? How close is my inside support? Am I going for the line?
- Shall I run through the defender by running straight? Is my opponent a light or powerful player? How close is

SWERVE, SIDE STEP, KICK AHEAD, 2 v 1 AND 2 v 2

Activity	Key learning points

A defender anticipates where the tackle will occur by the speed and direction of the ball carrier. The ball carrier has a range of decisions that depend on the defender's angle of approach and space available for evading the defender.

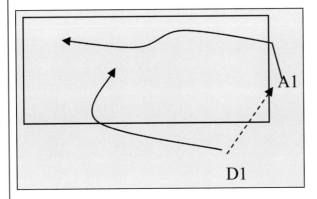

- D1 passes to A1. A1 attacks defender.

- A1 runs around cone into channel and has to score.

- D1 runs around cone and defends the channel.

Progression 1:
- Introduce chip/grub kick and chase.

Progression 2:
- Add another attacking player A2 so it becomes 2 v 1.

Progression 3:
- Add another defender D2 so it becomes 2 v 2.

ATTACKING WING
- The ball carrier slows down slightly to force the defender to change direction and choose a new line for the tackle

- Once the ball carrier sees a momentary hesitation in the defender, the ball carrier accelerates again (swerves) to score in the corner.

- If the defender's shoulders are parallel to touch-line, the ball carrier should side-step inside.

DEFENDING WINGER
- Defender to marshal the ball carrier towards the touch-line protecting own inside shoulder and checking the ball carrier will not get away on outside.

- **Progression 2:** the ball carrier should draw the defender before passing to the support player (on inside or outside).

- **Progression 3:** communication between two defenders is vital. Does D1 go for outside attacking player or take the first attacking player? How do the attacking players make it difficult for the defence?

my inside support? Am I going for the line?

- Shall I kick ahead? Is there no way I am going to beat my opponent? Is the support a long way off? Is there space behind my opponent to effectively chip the ball ahead?
- Shall I cut inside? Have I run out of space on the outside? Has the opposition covering defence arrived to cut off any step inside? Is it the best way to link with my support?

An ability to recognize impending isolation, and an understanding of the responsibility of avoiding a loss of possession, are tactical requirements of all good wings. It is acceptable to be tackled into touch when going for the corner and a possible try, but being tackled into touch after failing to decide to come in off the touch-line early enough is a major sin.

Entry from Blind Side as an Attacking or Decoy Option

The Blind-Side Wing should have licence to roam. By coming from depth, from behind the front-line attack and not necessarily where expected, the wing can pose defensive problems to the opposition. The Blind-Side Wing must be inside the ball at all times to keep all attacking options open. If 10 is tackled that winger will be the only player available to hit the ball from depth with pace; if 10 makes a half break, the winger can give it momentum from depth. The wing, therefore, must develop the ability to pass accurately up to approximately 15m from either hand while running at top pace.

The Deception Plan

The wing should not make it obvious where the strike will come by standing in the space between the Fly Half and first centre. The run

can be left until late, trailing the Fly Half and then arcing into the gap, being hidden behind the front-line attack.

The Fly Half should take the ball up to the opposition quickly, then slow and offer the pass to the receiver who is running at full pace. The Blind-Side Wing is starting 5–10m behind the Fly Half and will find it difficult catching up the Fly Half, if 10 continues sprinting away.

Space is created by the Fly Half, by stepping in and aiming at the inside shoulder of the first defender. This prevents the defender drifting into the gap to tackle the Blind-Side Wing.

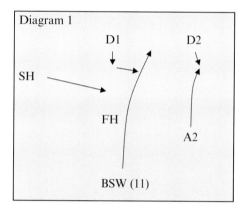

Diagram 1

The player on the other side of the gap steps out. If his defender stays on him, his shoulders will start to turn out and the Blind-Side Wing will be on the inside of D2's weak shoulder.

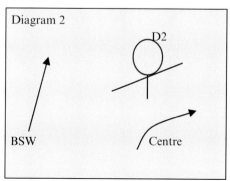

Diagram 2

The defending wing's angle of approach is wrong; he is not protecting his inside-shoulder. He will tackle the attacking wing should he go for the outside but…

…the attacking winger sees the defender's weakness and takes the inside channel with a side-step.

The swerve with ball in two hands disguises which way the player intends to go. The ball can be transferred to the far (left) arm to prepare the right for a hand-off.

This also creates another option for the Fly Half. If Defender 2 comes in to tackle the Blind-Side Wing, the Fly Half then passes to the unmarked First Centre (A2).

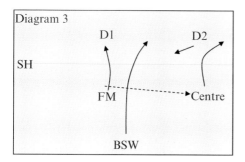

As part of the deception plan, the passer could dummy as if going for the break, and then make the pass. This should engage the first defender. FH could also look as though preparing to give a long pass. This will engage the attentions of the second defender, who will stay wide, marking the First Centre.

Alternative to the Deception Plan
It is also possible for the Blind-Side Wing to receive an inside pass from the first centre. This move will have the same objectives, but the intention is to deceive the defenders into believing the strike runner will be wider out because the Fly Half has made an early pass. The problem is that the first defender is now free to drift and cover the space the Blind-Side Wing is going to attack. The likelihood of a clean breakthrough is thus reduced.

Where and When: First Phase?
From a lineout, the Open-Side Flanker tends to mark the attacking Fly Half, allowing the defending Fly Half to cover any intrusion by the attacking Blind-Side Wing. For the attacking move to work, the defending back row needs to be engaged by a dynamic catch and drive to suck in the open side.

Scrums: for similar reasons, the scrum has

to nullify the defending Open-Side Flanker, either with a back-row move first or with a wheeling strategy. On the right side of the field the scrum goes up on the loose-head side, taking the open side away from the Fly Half; on the left side of the field, the scrum should go up on the tight-head side. With these scenarios, a man-for-man defence – Fly Half on Fly Half – takes over.

Where and When: Secondary Phases?
The secondary phase is probably the best time to use the Blind-Side Wing. The defence is disrupted, or organized with backs and forwards intermingled and on a man-for-man basis.

Where and When: Key Learning Points
- Timing: communication; running with purpose; appreciation of space/angles; depth of run; timing of run; options; fixing defenders; support play maintain impetus.
- Decoy running: always be a threat; 'interest' defenders; create chaos; create space for ball carriers or receivers.
- Strike running: get on line before the pass; be at full steam; have support organized to be on hand should penetration occur; action to take place as close to the tackle line as possible.

The Kicking Game

Long Kicking
The long kicking game has reduced the possibilities of the wings exploiting counter-attack if the flat line chase is well executed. There is still a need, however, to get the ball back up the field quickly.

If the ball is in front of the runner and space is available, the counter is an option. If this option is not available, it is safer to kick upfield

Continued on page 92

Activity: Passing off the shoulder

Key learning points

To emphasize the nature of the pass from Fly Half to Blind-side Wing and the running angles
- In 5s with a ball.
- 5 metre wide channel
- Single file

- Start one behind the other.
- Each player arcs out to receive a pass.
- Step in before passing to create space for receiver.
- Flat, soft, hanging pass.
- Feel the player running on to the pass

OBJECTIVES OF ACTIVITY: To develop timing of the run on to the pass and into the gap
- In 6s with a ball.
- To run down a channel 10 metres wide for 40-50 metres.
- 3 in front and 3 behind covering the gaps between the three in front.

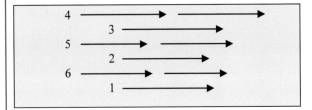

- Accelerate on to the pass as you come through the front line.
- Slow down before offering the ball to the line coming through.
- There is a cycle of acceleration and slowing down.
- Communicate to those in front where and when.
- Do not take up a position behind the gap you intend running into.
- Angle of run should be an arc to straighten the line.
- The pass should hang slightly

EXPLANATION:
- The three in front pass along the line to the end player.
- The other line surges through, receives ball, passes along line to end and first line comes through again.

Developments:
- In 5s , 3 jog forward continually passing the ball back and forth. 2 jog behind. 1 of these is to work while other rests.
- 1 decides where to enter the line, enters at pace and calling for ball then slows, the line reforms, passer going to back.
- The other player who started at back decides when and where to come into the line and takes place of the passer.

A. WINGER RETURN OF KICK DOWN TRAM-LINES

Activity: long kick

Players inside 5m to 15m tram-lines.
In 4s with ball.

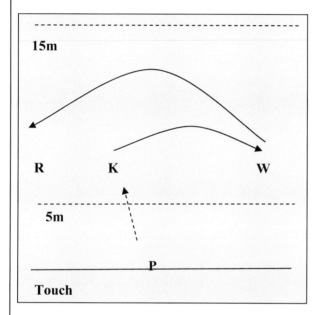

Explanation:
- Passer passes to Kicker who stands inside 5–15m channel.
- Kick chips to W 15m away.
- W gathers and returns long kick down tram lines to receiver
- Rotate – R to P; P to K; K to W; W to R

Extension:
- Add chasers.

Key learning points

CATCHING THE KICK
- Raise arms, spread fingers, relaxed palms facing up.
- Focus on ball.
- Catch ball with spread fingers.
- Pull ball down to chest and arms.
- Two hands on ball when hits chest.
- Hear thud of ball on chest.

Either END OVER END PUNT:
- Ball held slightly outside the line of the body.
- Hands release to side to drop ball in perfect position.
- Kicking foot planter flexed (toe pointing forwards).
- Head down and over ball.
- 'Chase' ball with foot, pulling whole body forward.
- Finish in front of kicking point.
- Right foot left hand or left foot right hand.

Or SPIRAL PUNT:
- Ball held slightly outside line of the body.
- Ball held at angle: right foot = 11 and 5, left foot = 1 and 7.
- Hands release to side to drop ball in correct position.
- Kicking foot planter flexed (toe pointing forwards), to create spiral motion.
- Head down and over ball.
- 'Chase' ball with foot.
- Finish in front of the kicking point.
- Right foot left hand, left foot right hand.

Continued from page 89

along the tram-lines (the 15-m channel). The requirement then is an accurate tram-line kicking technique that keeps the ball in play. This technique can also be used to clear the ball to touch.

High Ball Kick and Chase

When in doubt, when the options for running the ball back or kicking the tram-lines are not available, when there is a danger of being caught with the ball deep inside their own territory, wings should use the high-ball kick and chase. This will provide an opportunity for the ball to be won back.

Effective Kick Chase in a Sub-Unit

The wings must understand and work effectively with the outside backs in a sub-unit

when chasing diagonal kicks into space, box kicks and high balls.

Cross-Field Kick

The team will have developed an appropriate recognition and call for the cross-field kick, the 'forward pass'. The Open-Side Wing must take up the appropriate wide position and be adept at the catching technique, both in attack and defence. The wing should be wide and come from outside to inside, thereby facing the ball all the time.

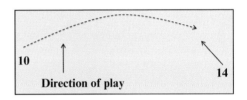

B. WINGER KICK AND CHASE

Activity: kick and chase

Key learning points

Receiving Team

- Team B be positive.

- Attack defenders to create 2 v 1.

- Attack gap – pull in defender and pass to space thus vacated.

Kick and chase:

- Quick chase.

- Move up talking in a straight line

- 4 v 3 in grid 20m long by 15m wide.
- Team A kicks ball (bomb) to attackers, chase and defend (two-handed holding tackles).
- Teams swap around.

C. KICKING TENNIS GAME TO PRACTISE THE BOMB

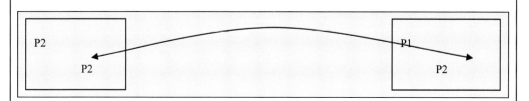

- 2 grids 10x10m with neutral zone of 20m between.
- Play 'tennis' by using the high kick.
- If caught, play on. If ball lands outside grid, play on.
- 1 point to the kicker if the ball hits the ground in opposition grid; if the ball is dropped in the grid; if the ball is caught but the catcher steps out.
- First to 10 points and best of three sets.

D. KICK CHASE AND RECEPTION (WIPER KICK)

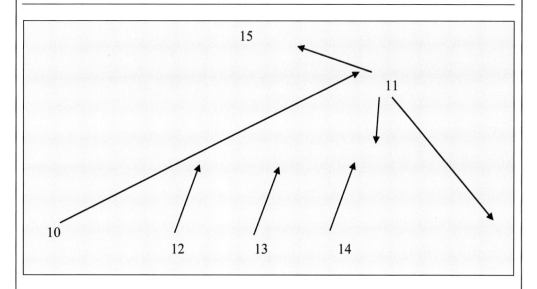

- 10 kick a diagonal either to or behind 11.
- 12, 13 & 14 provide an appropriate chase as a unit to limit the options for 11 who can run, pass to 15 or kick to touch.

Defending

A winger must be able to tackle. There is nothing so obvious on a rugby field as a wing who cannot tackle because most of the defensive situations are one-on-one in open play. The wings will be dealing with the opposition's most dangerous runners so the ability to tackle effectively and consistently in one-on-one defence is crucial. This is achieved by either closing the attacker down or using footwork to make an effective tackle in more confined areas. The majority of tackles will be arm tackles rather than shoulder tackles. This means that the attacking winger is trying to

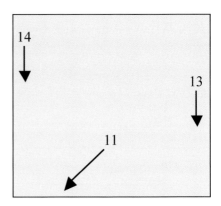

evade the tackle rather than run through the tackler.

A. THE TACKLE

Activity

Key learning points

Drill 1: *In pairs one with a ball, both on knees.*
Ball carrier is on knees and upright as tall as possible, ball held in two hands. He must at all times concentrate on control of the ball and his own body.
Tackler is on knees at 90 degrees to the ball carrier. Takes 4 tackles with the same shoulder, then the ball carrier turns through 180 degrees and the tackler repeats the 4 tackles with the opposite shoulder. Players swap roles.

Drill 2: *Back in pairs, both players on their feet.*
Set-up is the same as before and so is the action. Tackler now starts in a crouched position and concentrates on the technical aspects more than on the power of the hit.

Drill 3: *In groups of 5.*
Inside a 5x10m grid, tackler makes two tackles on the rest of the group who run at no more than 50 per cent pace down the channel. Ball carrier should, however, try to out manoeuvre the tackler inside the channel. When tackled, ball carrier must look to off-load the ball only when in control of his own body.

SIDE TACKLE
- Defend primarily with eyes and feet.
- Be determined.
- Eyes focus on target area (bottom of shorts).
- Hit with shoulder, with head behind the ball carrier (cheek to cheek).
- The arms should wrap the thighs followed by a tight grip, preferably hand on wrist.
- Tackler drives with the legs while holding on to the ball carrier until truly tackled to the ground.
- Roll away.

The winger also has to consider how to cut off the attacking wing to prevent the option of a pass from the Outside Centre. In the example, 11 has to try to legally block 14 from getting into a position to receive a pass from the attacking 13.

Activity	Key learning points

Drill 4: 2 v 2 in 10x10m grid

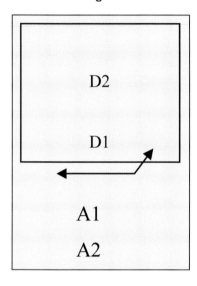

- A1 tries to lose D1.
- Defender 1 can only tackle when Attacker 1 crosses grid line.
- If tackled A1 off-loads and A2 has to beat D2.

Development:
- A1 gets back into game to make it
- D1 plays no further part in drill.

Key learning points

- When tackling from the side, tacklers should prepare by:
- Watching the ball carrier.
- Keeping head up, chin off chest, back flat.
- Concentrating on ball carrier's shorts.

Tackle is executed by:
- Putting head behind the ball carrier's legs – 'cheek to cheek'.
- Bracing shoulder, contact on thigh
- Wrapping arms around thighs, pulling and holding tight.
- Keeping eyes open.
- Driving up and through ball carrier with leg drive.
- Holding tight.
- Turning ball carrier sideways to land on top of ball carrier.

Off-loading out of contact:
- Power up – push through outside shoulder and hip.
- Ball carrier to lift ball up and away from body just prior to contact or brings ball into chest prior to bringing it off with two hands to make the pop.
- Knee, hip shoulder, ball – falling gradually

Passing off the ground
- Hits ground – two-handed pass.
- Chest pass like basketball.
- Push ball with sympathy.

B. BLOCKING

Activity

Key learning points

Drill 4: 2 v 1 in 20x15m grid

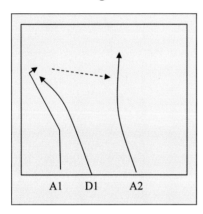

- One defender starts in line with the two attacking players.
- A1 starts to run with the ball, while defender D1 attempts to defend against A1 and A2 to prevent them from scoring.

- The attacking Outside Centre, A1, has beaten his opposite centre and made the inside shoulder of the defensive winger. The attacking Winger A2 has an overlap.

Objectives:
- To prevent the opposing Outside Centre providing an overlap for his wing.
- To force an error or an incomplete play for the attack

- Defending winger, D1, stays between the attacking Outside Centre, A1, and the attacking Winger A2.
- D1 runs with the centre, A1.
- D1 faces in towards the Outside Centre and remains between the Outside Centre and wing.
- In this position, it is possible to see any defending cross-cover coming to help.
- The defending winger lays off the Outside Centre and is not to be drawn to commit to the tackle until the point of no return, which is a question of judgement.
- So the defender isolates the ball carrier.
- Attackers should try to place themselves in a position where the pass will put the defender out of play.

Rear Tackle
- Be determined.
- Focus on the point of impact – the thigh.
- Both arms encircle the ball carrier and then slide down the legs.
- Tackles from behind should be made slightly from side on.
- Keep hold until the ball carrier is brought to the ground.

C. DRIFTING

Activity: Defence 2-3 on 1

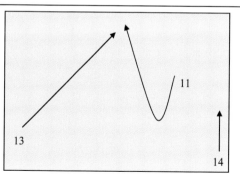

A3

A2

A1

14

Key learning points

- 14 works to get on attacker's inside shoulder and push the ball carrier out.

- Defender, 14, covers own inside shoulder so attacking player cannot step inside.

- 14 lines up in defence against 2 or 3 attacking players (A). First attacker has the ball and runs at 14.
- If first attacker does not pass then 14 tackles. If A1 passes then 14 will drift on to the next attacker and so on.
- The practice ends with a tackle by 14 on the ball carrier before the try-line

---

D. RETRIEVING BALL ON GROUND

Activity: Defence – retrieving ball on ground

11

13

14

Key learning points

- 11 to secure the ball on the ground by falling on it.

- Get back to feet quickly.

- Beat 14, 1 on 1.

- Or stay strong in the tackle to stay on feet as long as possible.

- 13 kicks the ball along the ground behind 11.
- 11 is under pressure from 14.

Progression:
- 15 introduced with less pressure from 14 so 11 has options to pass, run or kick.

Development of Specialist Physical Skills

Training Emphasis

Emphasis on training for wings will be on the following factors:

- Strength in contact – hit and spin; fending; bumping and leg drive; run, jump and catch under pressure.
- Speed endurance – continuous running in chasing kicks, covering back, supporting counter-attacks.
- Speed – develop good top running speed and accelerative speed to stop, turn and accelerate; jump, land and accelerate.
- Agility – ability to run in-lines and out-lines; side-step at variable pace; swerve then accelerate outside.

Example Training Sessions

Defence Agility

Take long recovery periods between runs to ensure quality and production of dynamic movements.

- Stop, turn and accelerate.
- Turn out to in.
- Run, jump and catch.
- Marshal defender on the outside.
- 5 of each with walk back recovery and 3 minutes between each movement.

Change of Pace and Direction
Individuals:

- Jog 3m and sprint 3m.
- Jog 3, sprint 2 left (right) and 1 straight.
- Jog 3m, sprint 3m left (right).

Pairs with ball:

- A v B. Ball on ground 3 paces in front of B. A to sprint, pick up, change direction left/right and add pace.

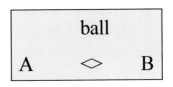

Development:

- B throws (lobs) ball to A.

Flat Speed

- 20–80m at 100 per cent speed with full recovery.
- Straight and arced runs.
- 2 x 3 sets x 40m and 1 x 2 x 80m.
- Walk back recovery.
- 6 minutes between sets.
- Fewer runs, more quality.

Flat Speed Endurance

- Any distance 40–110m.
- 3 x 4 sets x 50m, 30 seconds between runs, 5 minutes between sets
- Increase volume or reduce recovery.

Field Endurance

Running 'circuit' on the pitch including:

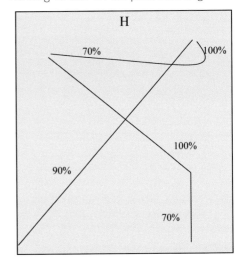

- long runs (70–80m);
- reaction accelerations;
- change of direction;
- side-step and swerve;
- 60–120 seconds between runs;
- runs 45–60 seconds at varying intensities;
- acceleration on the move.

Progression:
Maintain the quality but increase the volume.

Resistance Training Exercises

Weight Training
Develop both strength and power using the following specific exercises (using both free weights and elastic resistance): weighted sled, split-leg squat, high pull, low pull, hip flexion and hip extension, single-leg squat, lunge, lateral lunge, bent-over row, dips, pull-ups, horizontal row.

Plyometrics
Develop explosive strength with plyometric-type exercises. Take full recovery and minimal foot contacts per session. Add box jumps, single-leg hops, bounding.

Development of Specialist Mental Skills

Determination: 'A concentrated mind achieves more than strength alone.' Anon

The winger must be able to narrow in and block out distractions under pressure in a game. Wingers are often under-utilized and not as actively involved in the game as those players close to the action. In these circumstances, it can be difficult for a wing to maintain focus throughout the whole match and avoid a mental 'walkabout'. Distractions can occur, either in the crowd or in the player's own head, and these can have a

Pace is vital for a winger…

… and can always be improved.

detrimental effect on performance. The mind can misinterpret the visual and audible cues and fail to recognize what is and what is not relevant. The winger can then become a mere spectator, applauding the actions of his own team-mates and running around, but unable to get into the game and be effective.

It is possible to improve concentration skills by changing focus at the appropriate time, by establishing positional priorities at specific stages of play, by minimizing the distractions, and by maintaining the required focus throughout the whole period of the match.

The first step to improving the ability to focus and for long periods is to identify the shortfalls. What external factors intrude and distract the wing's attention? It might be a spectator shouting out a crass comment, or an opposition player ridiculing a mistake made by the wing. Having identified the causes and the points in the game at which the lapses of concentration occur, focus may be restored by the use of certain trigger words or phrases, such as 'the next play', 'focus on your opposite number', 'relax', depending on changing circumstances and personal needs.

Making a mistake should not weigh on a player's mind; instead, he must refocus on the next phase rather than be distracted by thoughts of why the mistake occurred.

Pre-match mental preparation is also important in enhancing concentration for the match. During this period, priorities for the match are identified, and perhaps even committed to paper as a reminder to be used in the changing room. Pre-match visualization also aids concentration. If, before a match, a player visualizes certain game situations and considers what decisions should be made in those situations, it is more likely that the correct decision will be made.

CHAPTER 6

THE FULL BACK (15)

Checklist of Positional Skills and Attributes

Technical

- Effective individual tackling technique off either shoulder.
- Ability to shadow and manipulate ball carrier.
- Ability to deal with opposition kicks of all types as a priority. Quality high-ball receipt skills under pressure (off the ground); whilst running; with feet firmly planted on the ground.
- Ball-gathering skills, with the ball rolling towards the player, as well as when turning to collect the ball rolling away from him.
- Kicking off either foot with accuracy and length, both as an attacking option and to relieve pressure. Variety is key.
- Goal-kicking and restarts are a plus.
- Long clearance pass.

Tactical

- Anticipation and ability to read the game.
- Good kicking awareness (punt for field position, bomb to recover ball and give forwards time to get back, chip as attacking weapon).
- Understanding of the requirements of counter-attack and the ability to execute them, and get the ball (and preferably a ball carrier) in front of the team as quickly as possible.
- Capacity to be the key attacking player from set and phase play, running with confidence and daring.

Physical

- Footwork/agility (side-step, swerve, acceleration, power).
- Ability to step off either foot at pace, and to change pace.
- Strength (in both upper and lower body) is needed to fend off chasing, would-be tacklers and to stay up in the tackle. This gives support players time to get back and help out.
- Height can be beneficial when fielding the high ball, but may be a disadvantage when lifting a ball from the ground. For the latter, flexibility (lower back and hamstrings) is desirable.
- Good hand–eye co-ordination
- Timing into back line with lines and with power and speed.

Mental

- Physical courage.
- Ability to see wider picture quickly.
- Sense of adventure.
- Confidence.
- Decisiveness.
- Calmness.
- Stability.
- Communication skills and ability to show leadership within the back three.
- Panoramic vision of the game: anticipate, scan, act, communicate.

The Specialist Role of the Full Back

The ideal Full Back is the complete rugby player, excelling in each of the generic skills of tackling, handling, kicking and running. The position demands a combination of the perception and kicking skills of the Fly Half with the evasion skills of the wingers and a Full Back has the ability to play in either of these positions. In both defence and attack, the Full Back operates in a mini unit with the two wingers.

Operating behind the front-line attack and first-up defenders, the Full Back's field of vision is wider than that of other players. Another advantage is having more time and space than any other player on the field. With good communication skills, the Full Back should be organizing both attack and defence.

The Full Back needs a well-developed positional sense, to be a good defender and to deal with opposition kicks. Being in the right position involves anticipating the opposition Fly Half's intentions. When the opposition are in possession deep inside their own 22, the Full Back should stand opposite their Fly Half; as play progresses downfield, the Full Back will get progressively wider, to defend against the running game and the diagonal kicks. The Blind-Side Wing will cover box kicks behind the forwards.

Generally in defence, from most phases, the Full Back is about 15m behind the midfield players, following the passage of the ball along the line, staying just inside the ball. From lineouts, the Full Back will cover the gap between the centres and then between the second centre and Open-Side Wing. The Blind-Side Wing will be between the Fly Half and the first centre.

From a midfield scrum, the Full Back will take up a central position. For a scrum near his own goal-line, the Full Back may take the short side depending on the defensive arrangements of his team. If the scrum is 15m in from either touch, the Full Back will take up a position behind and between the centres. From kick-offs and restarts, the Full Back will tend to be on the side of the field where the ball is likely to land, but generally to the centre of the field.

When defending the goal-line, the Full Back takes up a position directly behind the defence to deal with any kicks through or over the defence. The Full Back may, however, be required to be in the back line as one of the first-up defenders and covering the opposition 15. Again, it depends on the situation, so anticipation plays a significant role in determining the Full Back's positioning.

A good understanding of the game and good tactical decision-making make the complete Full Back.

Development of Specialist Technical and Tactical Skills

Joining the Attack

Due to a deep starting position behind the front-line attack, the Full Back's movements are partially hidden. This means a greater impact when joining the attack and provides an element of surprise. It allows a variation to the place of entry into the attack, and a change of pace, angle and numbers in the attack.

The channels between the Fly Half and the first centre tend to be where the Blind-Side Winger gets involved, so the Full Back tends to enter the line between the Outside Centre and wing or outside the Open-Side Wing. Entering the back line can create overlaps and contribute to an outflanking movement. The Full Back can exploit the short side from scrums and any that develop from a lineout by calling for a pass from the Scrum Half. A

JOINING THE ATTACK

Activity

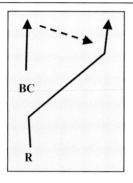

- In pairs. Ball carrier in front, runner behind like truck and trailer.
- Ball carrier jogs ready to give appropriate pass at correct time.
- Runner jogs 5m behind ball carrier and decides when to accelerate on to a pass and where and how wide.
- After receiving pass, swap roles

Development 1:
- In groups of six with a ball. Three players in front and three behind.
- Run along channel 10m wide by 40m long.
- Front three pass along line to end player.
- Other line surges through, receives ball, passes along own line to the end.
- First line comes through again.

Development 2:
- Four jog along channel 10m wide over 100m, continually passing the ball. Two players jog behind. One works, other rests.
- Working player decides where to enter the line at pace, then returns ball to line and gets back into position behind the line.
- 2 now comes into the line.

Key learning points

- Runner takes the decision which side of ball carrier to run and how wide.
- Direction and length of pass is communicated to ball carrier.

- Slow down before offering the ball to the line coming through to emphasize the change of pace.
- Accelerate on to the pass.

- Communicate where and when to those in front.
- Do not run behind gap you intend running into.
- Angle of run should be an arc.
- Runner straightens up as soon as he hits line.
- Offer soft, hanging pass.

team can create a good attacking situation from inside their own 22 because the opposition Full Back will take up a deep position to cover an expected long kick.

The 15 must understand his positional role in the attacking movement and consider the following questions: Am I to be the main strike runner, the decoy or a link in the passing movement? Am I coming in at pace to penetrate, or am I to arrive in a more controlled fashion to catch and pass the ball after fixing a defender? When entering the attack the Full Back should consider the following:

- he should not over-crowd the channel of attack;
- he should not slow the attack by adding an extra pair of hands that are not needed;
- he should not make it obvious where the run will be made;
- if he enters the line late the defence will have little time to react;

There must be a contingency plan, a fail-safe, in case the ball is turned over and the Full Back is not in position. Who will be covering if the ball is dropped and subsequently hacked through by the opposition? Does the Blind-Side Winger cover the Full Back or is everyone committed to the attack, trusting to their speed of reaction if they need to rush back?

Fielding Kicks

Attacking sides look to move the ball to space. If a defending side has spread its defences across the field so that there is no lateral space, one tactical option open to the ball carrier is to kick the ball into the space behind the defence. The Full Back's responsibility is to deal with this. The Full Back will have to deal with a number of tactical kicks.

The Bomb or High Ball

The Full Back must be safe under the high ball and this often requires courage. The chaser will be hoping to get the first touch, leaving the ground and then knocking the ball back to a support player. The Full Back, under such pressure, must jump to take the ball early. One advantage of jumping for the ball is that it is against the laws of the game to tackle a player while he is in the air.

The Punt

The punt is useful when a team wants to relieve pressure. It will attempt to do this by kicking long, down the 15-m channel, and organizing its chase to prevent a counter-attack. If a counter-attack is stopped at source, the side not in possession will be going forward and hoping for a turnover. The

Catching the high ball: concentration, palms upwards, stable base.

FIELDING KICKS

Activity	Key learning points

Activity

Exercise 1: catches with both feet on ground. Catcher has time, the chaser is not close enough to compete for the ball.
In pairs with ball.
Face each other, 10m apart.
1 throws to 2 – overarm and end over end.
2 catches.

Development 1:
1 now chip kick.
Development 2:
15–20m apart. High kick.

Exercise 2: catching under pressure. Chaser is close but cannot compete for the ball.
In 3s with shield and ball.
1 throws; 2 catches; 3 with shield gives small dig to receiver after he catches.

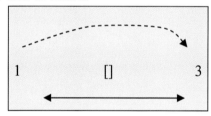

Development 1:
Kick higher and increase pressure from shield holder.

Exercise 3: leaving ground.
Chaser is close and would tackle the catcher, if the catcher remains on the ground.
In pairs with ball.
10m apart.
High throw, to land half-way between the pair.
2 runs to meet ball and in the air.

Development 1:
15–20m apart.
Now kick instead of throwing ball.

Key learning points

Preparation
- Lead with one arm and leg.
- Catcher is side on to attacker.
- Call 'my ball' to communicate intentions.
- Move feet to get into position.
- Create wide base with legs (shoulder width apart) to ensure balanced position and a position in which catcher will be able to jump to catch the ball if under extreme pressure.

Execution
- Raise arms, spread fingers, relaxed palms facing upwards.
- Focus on ball.
- Catch ball with spread fingers.
- Pull ball down to chest and arms.
- 2 hands on ball when hits chest.
- Hear thud of ball on chest.

Follow-through
- Sink hips to stable crouch.
- Sideways stance with shoulders braced.
- Maintain control of ball.

BALL – CHEST – ARMS
- Hold run – anticipate the flight and landing spot of the ball.
- Catch ball at highest point of the jump (peak).
- One knee up as protection.
- Square on for strong grip, otherwise any spillage will be a knock-on.

Activity	Key learning points

Exercise 4: catching under pressure.
In 3s with shield and ball.
1 throws; 2 catches off ground; 3 with shield gives small
dig to receiver after he catches.

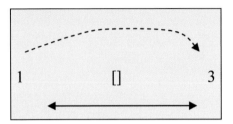

Development 1:
Kick higher and increase pressure from shield holder

Exercise 5: fielding ball on ground.
- Coach places or rolls ball behind FB into the 22-m area. 15 has to turn, collect ball and find touch aiming at a target grid.
- Practise both sides of field using left foot to left touchline because it is shielded from pressure from a chaser.

Development:
- Add a chaser to apply some pressure.

- Practise different ways of collecting ball.
- Fall on it, or trap with foot to avoid knock-on, or one hand to calm ball down and collect; or, kneeling, allow ball to roll into cradle of arms.
- One in the air as running back, collecting it over shoulder.

Full Back should never get caught with the ball behind the forwards if the opportunity is available to find touch first.

The Chip/Grubber Kick

The chip or grubber kick is intended to be re-gathered by the kicking side. Usually, the defenders who collect these kicks tend to be the sweepers from the first-phase ball – the Blind-Side Wing or Scrum Half. If the kicks go too long, the Full Back will have to field them under pressure.

Kicking

The Full Back must be capable of executing a variety of kicks, from the punt to touch or downfield deep into opposition territory to the high kick. The latter helps the Full Back avoid being caught behind the forwards, gives his team the chance to recover possession by chasing the ball, and allows the forwards time to get back between the ball and their own goal-line. The ability to kick off either foot is desirable when under pressure to find touch, to give the forwards time to regroup. A team's goal-kicker tends to be either the Full Back or the Fly Half, both chosen for these positions because of their kicking skills.

Punt to Touch or Deep Downfield: End-Over-End Technique

The ball is held slightly outside the line of the body, which enables a greater swing of the kicking leg. The hands are released to the side, allowing the ball to drop in the correct shape. (Throwing the ball up or pushing it down will force a deviation from the desired kicking shape.) The head is over the ball and the player looks down on striking the ball. He kicks through and beyond the ball, then follows through, left

Spiral kick: eyes on ball, tight left shoulder keeping hips square, good back swing with kicking leg, plant foot pointing at target.

hand to right foot (right-footed kickers), or right hand to left foot (left-footed kickers). The movement is continued forward after the kick, using body momentum for extra power and distance.

Punt to Touch or Deep Downfield: Spiral Technique

The ball is held slightly outside the line of the body, at 1 and 7 o'clock for a right-footed kicker, or 11 and 5 o'clock for a left-footed kicker. Dropping the ball from this position, not a slicing kicking action, will create a spiral. The hand is released to the side, almost as if placing the ball on a shelf, and the ball is then released (not thrown up or pushed down). As for the end-over-end technique, the head is over the ball and the player looks down on striking. He kicks through and beyond the ball, then continues the forward momentum after the kick.

Goal-Kicking

The ball is aligned on a kicking tee with the seam pointing to the middle of the posts. The exact position will be specific to individuals, dependent on approach, strike, habits, and so on. A slow, calculated approach is best. Power comes from the last step, not a pacey approach to the ball. Focusing on the point of contact on the ball, not the target, will keep the head down. Shoulders are kept tight in a coil, ready to open on contact with the ball. The non-kicking foot should be aligned straight towards the posts. The kicking foot comes straight from six inches behind the ball, strikes the ball, and then follows straight through for another six inches towards the target. The head must stay down and over the ball on contact. The shoulders turn to face the posts on contact, then hold straight in the follow-through. The kicker should follow through forward and towards the target, never fall away after the strike.

A. PUNTING PROGRAMME: SPIRAL OR END-OVER-END KICK

Take 5 kicks from goal-line in channel between 5-m and 15-m lines. A successful kick must land inside the channel. How far are these kicks? Measure up to where they land. If they roll and stop inside the channel, measure up to where the ball came to rest.

Date	Kick 1	Kick 2	Kick 3	Kick 4	Kick 5	Total
1						
2						
3						
4						
5						
6						
7						
8						
9						
10						

Punting: Key Factors

End-Over-End Punt
- Ball held slightly outside the line of the body.
- Hands release to side to drop ball in perfect position.
- Kicking foot plantar flexed (toe pointing forwards).
- Head down and over ball.
- 'Chase' ball with foot pulling whole body forward.
- Finish in front of kicking point.
- Right foot left hand, or left foot right hand.

Spiral Punt
- Ball held slightly outside the line of the body.
- Ball held in correct position: right-footed kicker, 11 and 5 o'clock; left-footed kicker, 1 and 7 o'clock.
- Hands release to side to drop ball in correct position.
- Kicking foot plantar flexed (toe pointing forwards), to create the spiral motion of the ball.
- Head down and over ball.
- 'Chase' ball with foot.
- Finish in front of the kicking point.
- Right foot left hand, or left foot right hand.

B. PLACE-KICKING PROGRAMME

Take kicks from each of the above positions.

		date	date	date	date	date	date	date	date
POS	QTY								
1	5								
2	5								
3	5								
4	5								
5	5								
6	5								
TOT	30								

Left-footed spiral kick: feet pointing towards target.

Place Kick: Key Factors

- The ball must be placed in an appropriate position (never leaning back), and with the seam lined up with the middle of the posts. The seam is seen as the target.
- The ball is kicked below the centre, making sure that the strike is not too low, which will lead to back spin and reduced distance.
- The run-up is shorter rather than longer and the approach to ball is slow.
- A 60-degree approach to the ball allows good leg power.
- The kicker comes straight on to the ball.
- The last step is of major importance. The non-kicking ankle should be opposite the ball and about 30cm (12in) away. Every player must practise in order to determine his own best distance.
- The power in the strike comes from the last step. A bigger step ought to impart more power than a shorter one, but there is a point at which that last step becomes too long and the power decreases. Timing will beat sheer power for distance.
- The standing foot points towards the target (helping bring body through straight).
- Head is down and over the ball.
- The foot comes through 15cm (6in) straight in front of ball.
- The foot will strike in plantar flexion (in other words, toe away from ankle).
- The foot is to chase the ball through straight; it must be straight 15cm (6in) after the strike.
- Even after the strike, the kicking foot remains aimed at the posts. If the kicker topples left or right after contact, it will probably be the planted foot that is responsible because it is pointing to one side or the other. The planted foot should be pointing at the target throughout the action.
- The leg action follows right through towards the line of strike, and the head stays down.
- The body weight is maintained on the non-kicking foot so that everything can come through the line of the ball. The kick ends up in front of the kicking point with the body pointing towards target.
- The chest should be square on to the ball.

Place kick: long last stride, plant foot pointing at posts, eyes concentrating on ball.

C. FULL BACK DECISION-MAKING AT KICK RECEPTION

Organization:

- 3 players A, B, C each in a grid. 3 grids coned in separate colour codes – 1 in blue on half-way kick off spot; 1 (green, yellow) on each of tram-lines at half-way.
- Kicker kicks to opposition wings and Full Back stationed in their own 22m.
- X opposition with shield.
- Y opposition without shield.
- Kicker with a supply of balls on half-way midfield spot.
- Receivers to communicate where the space is and get the ball kicked to that grid.
- Decisions revolve around who is in best position to make kick.

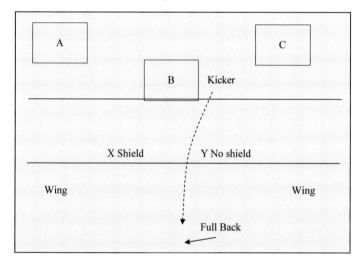

Activity explanation:

- Kicker kicks to FB.
- Coach calls options – kick to blue (red, yellow) – and FB responds.
- Coach calls 'pressure' and bag holder quickly opposes – FB must be safe under high ball.
- 'Runner' – opposition without shield chases – FB to beat him with footwork or chip.
- 'Pass' – pass left or right to nominated winger (to beat runner).
- 'Pass 2' – FB to use both wings to beat pressure and runner.

Initiating Counter-Attack

With a positive attitude and self-confidence in his own ability, a Full Back can launch counter-attacks from the opposition's deep kicks, long 22 drop-outs or long kicks at goal. Sometimes the Full Back will have to field a high ball, sometimes it means retrieving a ball rolling on the ground. Sometimes the Full Back will be faced by a broken field, sometimes by a well-organized chase. In the face of all these factors, a decision whether to run, kick or pass will have to be taken. One priority is to avoid being caught in possession and isolated, with team-mates unable to get back to offer support.

The Full Back will operate with the wings, who are deeper than the midfield and can usually get back to help out. There will have to be communication between the three and some form of organization or movement pattern in place (see Chapter 8, on 'Back-Three Play'). If fielding the ball under pressure, the Full Back does not have the peripheral vision of any support player. In this case, it is the support player who is the decision-maker, acting as the eyes and ears of the Full Back. However, if the ball is caught cleanly and in space without immediate opposition pressure, it is the Full Back who decides whether to kick or to launch a counter-attack.

Last Line of Defence

The Full Back is in the last line of defence and responsible for organizing it in the eventuality

---

Activity: Support communicating with fielder

Exercise 1:
- In 5s on goal-line. Limit size of channel to 15-20m wide.
- Coach rolls ball 8–10m. 1 of the 5 is nominated to defend the goal-line as the other 4 drop back to field the ball and counter-attack.
- Defender chases and defends on the coach's command.
- 4 attackers get back.

Exercise 2:
- A1 throws ball to B1 and chases to oppose.
- B1 runs back at A1 and works with C1 to beat him with a switch or off-load early if under pressure (high ball).
- Rotate: A joins queue B, and so on.

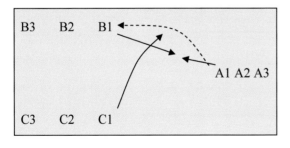

Key learning points

- Nearest retrieves ball in most appropriate manner.
- Specific communication from support, such as 'You have time; turn and bring ball forward,' or 'Man on, pass now, wide right,' and so on.

- Support to be eyes of ball retriever.
- Communicate when to pass.
- Bring ball forward quickly (loop/switch).
- Fix chaser.

Activity: Wing and Full Back relationship

Key learning points

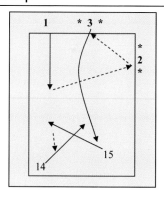

1 runs to end of grid, passes to 2 who passes to 3. 3 kicks to wing, who works with FB to launch counter-attack move.
- Pass and loop.
- Switch.

Rotate 1 to 3; 3 to 2; 2 to 1; 14 and 15 swap roles.

Exercise 4:
- In 3s in successive waves over a channel of 22-m width. Coach kicks ball and they counter-attack in set patterns:
  - o BSW gives long pass to FB, who runs towards coach but gives a switch to the BSW going towards the open.
  - o FB receives kick and switches with BSW after running back towards kicker; BSW links with OSW.
  - o OSW receives kick and runs towards kicker, dummy switches with FB and switches with BSW.

- Bring ball forward quickly.
- Support communicates with retriever.

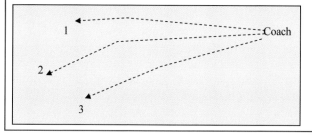

Last Line of Defence

Exercise 1:
The defending wings and full backs work in pairs.
The defending wing A kicks the ball to the attacking wing C.
Defending wing chases to tackle the receiver.
Receiver tries to evade tackle. If successful, the Full Back B tries to tackle the attacking wing.
Wing can only score in the 15m-wide channel.

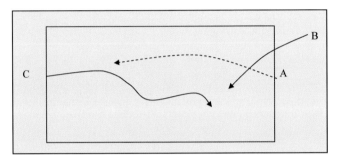

of a breakthrough or outflanking movement. Any player who has broken through or gone around the defence has to be closed down and tackled. The initiative has to be re-gained by reducing the ball carrier's thinking time and the approach work has to be at an angle that limits the ball carrier's options. While protecting the inside shoulder, the Full Back will marshal the attacker towards the touch-line and tackle at the best possible moment.

Development of Specialist Physical Skills

Kicking When Fatigued

As with the wings, top speed is important. In order to be effective at top speed the Full Back needs sufficient strength to have the confidence to come into contact at pace. Most importantly, he must possess a dynamic evasive side-step, off both feet. The Full Back

attacks over distances of 20–60m, with the potential to run the whole length of the field, either with the ball in hand or a combination of this and support running. Defensive running is mostly between 10–40m, working with the wingers to cover the width and length of the field. Such repeated, relatively long runs demand a high aerobic base, which will allow a good recovery from each bout of work.

Besides all this work, with or without the ball, the Full Back also has to retrieve the ball and kick for distance or to touch. The 15 can also be the team's goal-kicker. Games can be won or lost by the effectiveness, or otherwise, of the kicker. However, individual kickers rarely practise under the right circumstances, and this may result in a poor kicking performance during a game. To carry out a specific motor skill with success in a match, a player must replicate the game situation in training. The kicker does have time in a match

Shuttle sprint – 1 minute

5m between each cone:
- Start at cone 1.
- Sprint forwards to cone 2. Run backwards to cone 1.
- Sprint forwards to cone 3. Run backwards to cone 1.
- Sprint forwards to cone 4. Run backwards to cone 1.
- Sprint forwards to cone 5. Sprint forwards to cone 1 and start again.

Agility drill – 1 minute

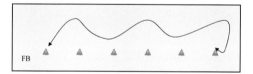

1.5m between cones
- Sprint through the cones.
- At the end cone, spin around and come back through the cones.

Tackle drill – 1 minute

1m between each tackle bag.
Middle one lying on ground
- Jump over the middle tackle bag 3.
- Tackle bag 1.
- Get up quickly, jump over bag 3.
- Tackle bag 2.
- Continue.

to compose himself, place the ball on the tee, assess the weather conditions, block out distractions, and take the kick, but he may well have run 40–80m at top speed just moments before. Even the time allowed for preparation for the kick may be insufficient for recovery. In addition, if the player himself scored the try, his mind may still be going over the moment, and the adrenalin will still be pumping.

Practising place kicks in training without being fatigued will fail to replicate the demands of the game of rugby. It is easy to be led into a false sense of security by practising in more favourable conditions. The chances are that the individual who has trained specifically and under pressure will be the one who gets the ball between the uprights, to clinch a match in the final minute of extra time with a conversion, penalty or drop kick.

Conditioning Drills

A more realistic game situation can be created in training by setting up the conditioning drills and completing one drill before each kick that is attempted. The players works for one minute at maximal intensity during each drill and allows a minute to complete the individual kicking routine. The number of successful attempts out of the twelve kicks taken while fatigued is recorded on the 'Place-Kicking Programme'. Every kick should be taken from one of the six designated spots.

Development of Specialist Mental Skills

Confidence

'Besides pride, loyalty, discipline, heart, and mind, confidence is the key to all the locks.' Joe Paterno

As the last line of defence and a player responsible for covering a large area of the field, the accomplished Full Back must be calm under pressure and confident. A team well versed in the strengths and weaknesses of the opposition Full Back can easily exploit any frailties and destroy the player's confidence.

Arguably, confidence has the greatest influence on sport performance. Players gain confidence from previous good performances (success breeds success). The role of the coach is also valuable in enhancing self-confidence and practice can be organized in order to promote successful outcomes. Structured goal-setting can also promote confidence. The key principles of goal-setting are well documented and a combination of outcome, performance and process goals can be highly effective. If goals are to be used to enhance self-confidence, however, they must be set at appropriate difficulty levels.

A player can develop confidence through seeing another player perform successfully and then modelling himself on the other's achievements. This may be done by using imagery/visualization in the pre-match period and during performance to visualize the next situation or skill required. Verbal persuasion can also manipulate behaviour. A coach can play a big part in confidence-building by using positive feedback and encouraging comments.

Emotional arousal, when perceived positively by the player, can also increase levels of confidence. In order to enhance self-confidence through this component, relaxation strategies can be adopted to reduce any perceived over-arousal. The opposite – in other words, activation strategies – can be practised for use in situations when arousal levels are perceived to be too low.

Composure

Emotions play a significant role in sport. Many things happen during a match, from unforced errors (for example, missing the easy kick in front of goal), to a referee's decision that may be perceived to be unfair or bad (for example, the call for a 'mark' not being heard and play being allowed to continue). The way in which a player responds to such situations may have a direct effect on performance. There are many examples of performers being unable to control their emotions, from a lack of confidence to over-confidence, resulting in complacency or excessive debilitative anxiety. Players need to learn how to control their emotions by focusing on the things they can control and on their own personal goals.

CHAPTER 7

MIDFIELD PLAY

Setting the Attacking Structure of the Back Line

Alignment

Over the years, much has been said about the alignment of the back line – that is to say, the space between players, and the depth and angle that the backs take up in relation to the gain-line and source of possession. The alignment depends on the experience or maturity of the players, their skill levels and what the attack wants to achieve. The decisions relating to alignment should be based on the particular situation each time – none is wrong and the choice must be circumstantial.

Gain-Line and Tackle Line

The gain-line is an imaginary line across the pitch running parallel to the goal-lines. It runs through the middle of the scrum and lineout and phase play – where the ball is when put in or stopped. If the attacking side gets the ball across this imaginary line, it has gained ground and is going forwards. Going forwards to the ball

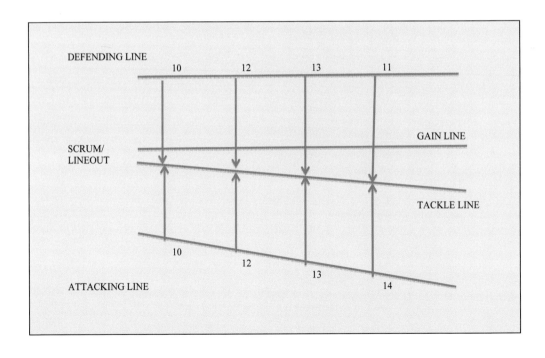

rather than having to recycle it by going backwards is not only easier but is also one of the principal aims of the game. A team should always be looking to go forwards.

The tackle line is another imaginary line across the field, not necessarily parallel to touch. It is the line that takes shape when the two lines – the attacking line and the defending line – collide. Assuming both lines are approaching each other at the same speed, the tackle line means that the attacking line does not reach the gain-line purely because the attacking line starts deeper behind the gain-line than the defenders. From a lineout the defenders line up level with each other and 10m back where the off-side line is set. The attackers cannot pass forward so they line up staggered, and this is the alignment.

There is a relationship between the depth at which the Fly Half receives the ball from the Scrum Half and the options: stand deep to kick for ground; stand flatter if executing a tactical kick; if passing in attack, interest defenders by taking the ball flat; if moving the ball wide, it is necessary to consider whether the next player can get his pass away the distance between the attacking line and the defenders. The further along the line the ball has to be passed, however, the deeper 10 will have to take the ball. The distance away from the defenders that the Fly Half makes passes also affects the whole back line. If the passes are deep and a long way from the opposition, the defenders can drift easily and their defensive duties are made easier.

Angle

The attacking structure is also affected by the angle at which the Fly Half runs. If he runs at right-angles to the line of pass, it is easier to receive the Scrum Half's pass, but then the Inside Centre must be responsible for straightening the line by standing wide and running in a straight line. It is better if the Fly Half is on a straight running line initially, to interest the opposition and hold them close in.

Stationary or Running?

Should the Fly Half take the ball standing still or running on to it? If he is running on to the pass, the distance between the attacking and the defending line is reduced, putting pressure on the outside players but also interesting defenders. If 10 receives the ball standing still, the back row and opposite number lose interest and drift on to the centres. If 10 is used as a pivot, the Inside Centre becomes the decision-maker. Some sort of movement is necessary to interest the defenders but not so much as to make life difficult for the centres. The Fly Half should move when the ball is in the Scrum Half's hands, but take care not to creep forward before then. From second phase he can take the ball at pace. The key is to add variation.

Midfield Movement Patterns

There are a number of typical movement patterns in the midfield that are used to unbalance defences – the strike runner being tailed by the Blind-Side Wing looking for the off-load. The use by the midfield of a fourth attacker (Blind-Side Wing or Full Back), coming from a different area and creating a different point of attack, increases the options and the range of movement patterns.

SETTING THE ATTACKING STRUCTURE OF THE BACK LINE (ALIGNMENT)

Activity	Key learning points

Realignment:
- Back line to attack goal-line from 22-m line.
- On whistle, put ball down.
- Nearest player acts as SH, the rest realign.
- Ball played after count of 3.
- Go in same direction twice – realign to come back other way.

Development 1:
- Build in a switch or loop or cut-out pass.

Question: How much time can I give outside men to do something?

Development 2:
- Ball carrier to decide and call out what is to happen, such as 'switch' or 'come and take ball' or 'looping' or 'cut pass'.

- Do not be lazy.

- Do not get flat.

- See number of player on inside.

Development 3:
- Backs support backs. Coach shouts instructions: 'down', 'tackled', or 'breakthrough'.
- 'Down': nearest player goes in and acts as SH.
- 'Tackled': nearest back goes in to help and rips ball away and play is continued.
- 'Breakthrough': accelerate for 5m; support gets there quickly and calls for pass.

- Do not overrun ball carrier.

- Call for ball.

Development 4:
- Coach insists on cut pass or loop or switch every time ball gets across gain-line.

Movement Patterns

This list is not definitive.
Change-Over
The two centres cross over, effectively swapping positions. The Fly Half passes to the First Centre (2) going wide.

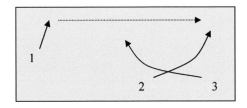

Activity: Quality of passing and fixing defenders

Key learning points

SH gives ball to first group of attackers. D1 goes for A1, D2 for A2.

Attackers to fix defenders and release overlap.

Coach shouts 'Break', 2 defenders run across grid to defend against second group of attackers.

SH then gives pass to second attacking line.

- Get outside shoulders pointing back towards source of ball: 'Get square'.

- Step in towards the ball: arc running'.

- Personal space – avoid bunching, tripping over each other; metre space around ball carrier.

- Come from depth and accelerate on to ball.

- Aim at inside shoulders of defenders to prevent them drifting.

- If no one in front run at defenders not away, to prevent drift.

- Pass at appropriate time – can the next attacker get his pass away?

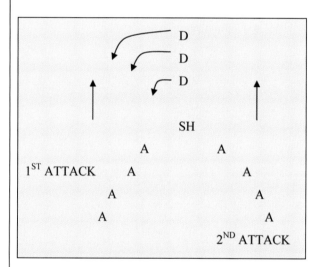

Change Under

Same as the previous play but the Fly Half passes to the Second Centre angling back – a short pass.

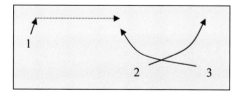

Change Blocker Over

Same as Change Over but the pass goes behind the Second Centre (3).

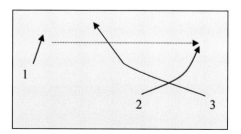

Miss 1, Loop 1

(Standard move) Fly Half passes long to the Second Centre. First Centre loops to receive a pass from the Second Centre

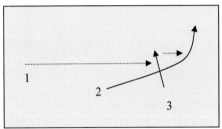

Return Switch

Fly Half and First Centre switch and First Centre gives a return pass to the Fly Half.

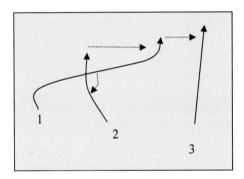

Return Switch Delayed

Fly Half and First Centre switch. First Centre gives a pass to the Second Centre angling back. Second Centre gives a pass to the Fly Half who has looped outside him.

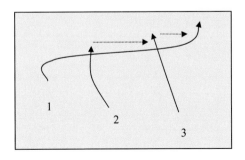

SIN (Switch Inside Pass)

First and Second Centres switch. Second Centre can pass inside to Fly Half.

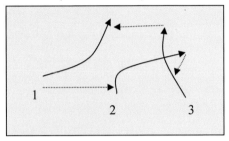

Two Ball Return Option

Fly Half switches with First Centre. First Centre has the option to return the pass to the Fly Half or to the Second Centre angling in or out.

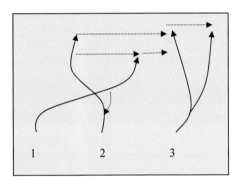

Yo-Yo

Fly Half passes to First Centre angling in. First Centre returns the ball deep to the Fly Half who is now directly behind the First Centre. First Centre is acting as a shield or blocker. Fly Half passes to Second Centre who is running on any one of three angles.

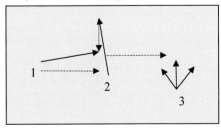

Rangie Option

Fly Half runs diagonally and First Centre runs a similar angle with him. Second Centre angles back, offering a switch option for the Fly Half. Fly Half either passes to Second Centre on the switch or the First Centre on his outside.

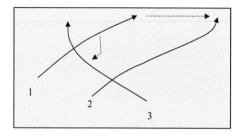

Reverse Rangie

Fly Half gives a long pass to Second Centre, who runs back across the face of the First Centre and Fly Half. He gives the pass to the Fly Half, who passes out to the First Centre.

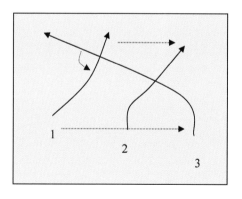

LIP (Loop 1, Inside Pass)

Fly Half passes to First Centre and then loops. First Centre gives pass to Second Centre. Second Centre gives pass inside to Fly Half.

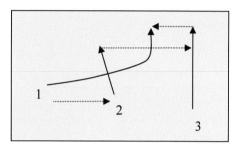

Double Switch

Fly Half gives pass to First Centre who switches with Second Centre. Second Centre now switches with Fly Half.

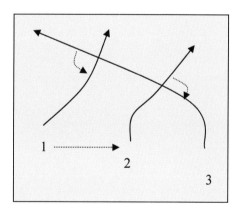

Miss 1, Loop 2

Fly Half gives long pass to Second Centre.

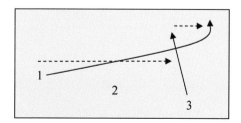

One Out Blocker Over

Fly Half to First Centre then loop outside Second Centre. First Centre passes to Fly Half behind Second Centre. Second Centre angling in.

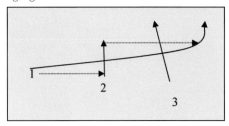

Flying Angel

Fly Half to First Centre. First Centre runs diagonally and dummy switches with Second Centre. First Centre passes inside to Fly Half on a diagonal run.

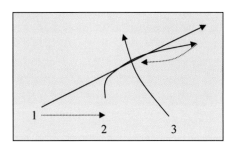

Pass, Pass Circle Ball

2 and 3 loop.

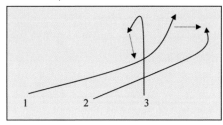

Key Learning Points

Successful accomplishment of these moves depends on the ability of each player to do the following:

- Execute a variety of passes off either hand with precision and correct timing.
- Understand the various roles of each player in the movement.
- Adopt the correct angles and timing of the various runs in switching and looping, unders and overs lines.
- Communicate which move is on.
- Be aware of space: how fast is the space disappearing between attackers and defenders? How much space between defenders is available for attack? How much personal space is there around the ball carrier (players must not trip over each other!)? How much space can be created by hooking defenders out of position?
- Know their targets: the inside or outside shoulder of the defender? The space between defenders?

Organizing the Defence

The Fly Half must be able to play a full role in defence as a tackler, and needs to be able to co-ordinate the back-line defence from set pieces and phase plays. The chosen defensive system depends on the team's game plan and the Fly Half is responsible for making it work. There are a number of various defensive systems that can be employed.

Position of the Opposition Fly Half

Observing the opposition Fly Half can help a team decide the way to defend. The positioning of the 10 will often be a clue to the attacking intentions of the opposition. If the intention is to kick, putting pressure on the Fly Half's strong foot can force a switch to the weaker foot, and the weakness may then be exploited.

If the Fly Half is standing flat, close to the gain-line, a straight-up rush defence may be used. The midfield should stand closer together and the defensive line speed should be very quick, with the midfield moving up quickly to pressurize the opposition into poor decisions.

If the opposition Fly Half stands deep, a drift defence may be employed. Every defender moves up and out so they are, in effect, tackling the man outside their opposite number. This forces attackers to run sideways.

Man-for-Man Defence

The midfield three (Fly Half and two centres) stay close. As they run towards the attacking midfield they adopt the 'hockey stick' approach. They come towards their opposite numbers from the inside shoulder, thus protecting any inside break and forcing the attack to see gaps on the outside.

The Fly Half should be leading the defending midfield following the ABC theory: A, Approach quickly; B, in Balance; C, then Close out. The Blind-Side Wing covers across, staying inside the ball, ready to tackle anyone breaking through. Initially the best place for the Blind-Side Wing to stand is in a triangular formation, with and near to the Fly Half and the Inside Centre.

The differences between the various forms of man-for-man defence revolve around the responsibilities of the outside players. The first form involves the Full Back taking the second last man and the Open-Side Wing taking the outside man. The Blind-Side Wing then covers deep for the Full Back. This might normally be used outside the defending team's own 22m zone. It can be called an isolation defence, because wing stays on wing, turning and running alongside the player to prevent the pass from the Full Back.

In the second form, the defending Open-Side Wing comes in to take out the attacking Full Back as he comes into the line. The Blind-Side Wing then sweeps behind the back line, and the Full Back takes the last player (the wing). This defence is adopted inside the defending team's own 22m zone (see below).

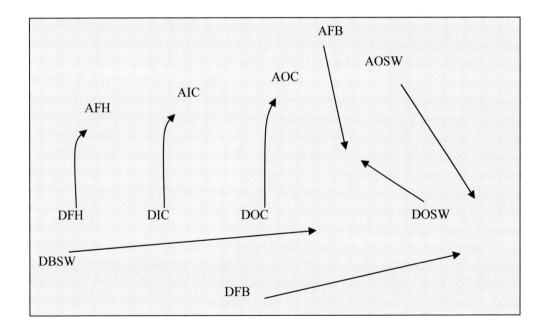

Drift Defence and One-Out Defence

In the drift defence the Fly Half stands opposite his opposing Fly Half and the rest of the midfield look as though they are playing man-for-man. With the one-out defence, the difference is the starting position – the Fly Half stands opposite the Inside Centre and the Inside Centre stands opposite the Outside Centre. The end result is that the Open-Side Flanker covers the attacking Fly Half, the Fly Half takes the Inside Centre, the Inside Centre takes the Outside Centre and the Outside Centre takes the Full Back. The Blind-Side Wing still covers any break. The line of run is like plugging the gaps: up–across–up.

In the approach work for the drift defence, the first couple of strides should be forward on to the opposite number. The defenders may have to employ a man-for-man defence if their Open-Side Flanker has been taken out of the game, for example, by having to tackle someone. All the defenders should wait for the call from the Fly Half to drift. If none is forthcoming, they play man-for-man. The call to drift will normally come if the attacking Fly Half passes straight away. If the Fly Half holds on to the ball, it is likely that the aim is to send someone through the midfield. In this case, players should not be sent out wide, as they will be needed to cover the inside channels.

Blitz (Rush) Defence

This type of defence is still man-for-man but the principle behind it is that each defender

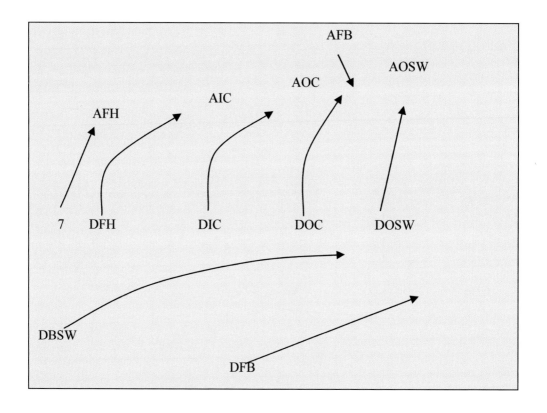

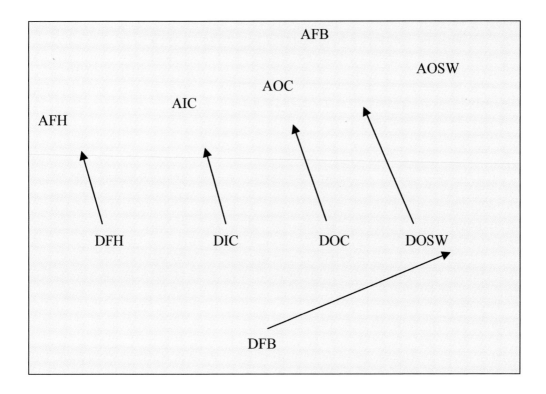

gets on the outside of his opponent and comes up fast in a line allowing him to make the tackle on his inside shoulder. This system means crossing the gain-line very quickly, thus denying the attackers time and space. It prevents the opposition going wide and around the defence and creates uncertainty in the mind of the attacking players, who are looking in the direction of the ball on their inside shoulder and cannot see the defenders approaching from their outside shoulder.

The main weakness of this defensive system is that, because of the speed of the line, defenders on the outside can sometimes get ahead of slower inside defenders, thus enabling the ball carrier to see the space and head for the gaps. This defence relies on the wing spotting or hitting in on the ball carrier, that is, being ahead of his insides, so it can also be vulnerable to the diagonal chip or grubber since there is always space behind the wing. The Scrum Half has to cover these kicks. Decoy runners may also confuse and isolate defenders; because the line is moving so quickly, there is little time to react and therefore it is more difficult to make the correct decision.

ORGANIZING THE DEFENCE

Activity	Key learning points

Defensive Technique Reaction: 2 v 1 and 3 v 2

Defensive reaction time – alignment under pressure – movement off line – footwork – defensive technique under pressure for both front and side tackles – defensive communication, listening and reacting.

Drill 1

Description:

- Defender starts lying face down with his head away from opposition.
- Coach blows whistle, defender reacts quickly to feet and moves off line. At same time attackers move forwards from their staggered positions.
- Coach calls '1' or '2' and defender reacts and tackles pad holder 1 or 2.

Drill 2

Description:

Progression with an extra defender and attacker. If coach calls '1', both defenders tackle first two pad holders. If coach calls '2', inside defender pushes outside defender out and defenders tackle pad holders 2 and 3. Grid 2 to add a communication and defensive pattern element

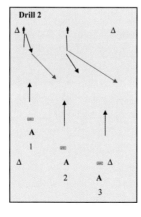

- Defenders align on inside shoulder of attackers before moving forwards.
- Defenders take first 4m straight up as quickly as possible before reacting to call of coach.
- On coach's call, defenders track hip of relevant attacker.
- Before contact, dip at knees with front foot as close to attacker as possible before driving up off front leg to engage maximum amount of leg drive.
- Defender's heads up and to side for front-on tackle, at back for a side tackle.
- Contact point for front-on tackle is shoulder in mid-drift, contact arm bound on to back, with arm hooking leg of attacker.
- Contact point for a side tackle is shoulder on quads.
- Second defender must align with some 'stagger' (a half body behind inside defender) and react to inside defender's push call if 2 called.

Skill development: Defensive organization M for M and drift

Key learning points

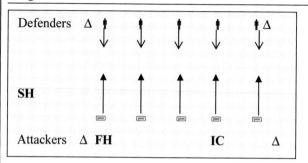

Defenders △   △

SH

Attackers △ **FH**   **IC**   △

Description:
- Man for Man defence.
- SH with ball at R/M situation. When SH passes to FH, attackers move up staggered and defenders make tackles.

Development:
- Drift/push defence.
- FH passes immediately to IC.

- Defenders go forwards.

- Inside defender communicates.

- Defenders push out.

129

Skill development: Defensive organization around R and M

Coaching points

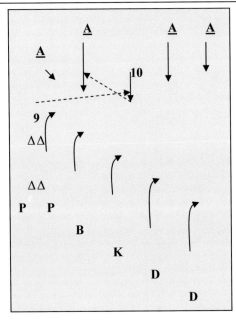

Description:

- Four cones placed in square formation to identify last feet of ruck for both sides.
- Attacking side except for 9 and 10 run with pads.
- 9 and 10 run game-specific lines and deliver the ball to support players running inside, switch, unders or overs lines.

Development:

- Once defence makes tackle, tackler/s and closest defender go down on one knee with attacker to form ruck.
- This sets the next offside lines.

Coach delivers second ball to 9, counts from 5 to 1. Whilst this occurs, both defence and attack re-align. Once count reaches 1, activity is repeated.

Variations:

- Different running lines by the attack to put pressure on the defence

- Post defenders align either side of the ruck, and set themselves at last feet.

- Block and key align half a step behind the defender inside them to adopt a staggered defensive line (particularly important with drift defensive).

- Key aligns with outside shoulder on inside shoulder of 10. Block aligns between post and key.

- Defenders outside key align on the inside shoulder of their opposite attacker, a half step behind the defender inside them.

- When 9 touches the ball, defenders move forwards.

- Roles: post takes pick and drive. If 9 runs, post looks to take 'S' ball runner on inside of 9. If 9 delivers to 10, post looks to take wide inside ball off 10 close to ruck.

- Block: takes 9 if 9 runs or 9 delivers the ball to 10, looks to take inside runner off 10.

- Key: defends against 10. Only when 10 delivers ball outside do any of inside defenders push to the ball.

CHAPTER 8

BACK-THREE PLAY

Counter-Attack

General Principles

Counter-attack is a means of turning defence into attack. It should be part of a whole-team philosophy that is concerned with how best to deal with turnover possession. The following core principles of counter-attack should be used by players and coaches to play what they see in front of them. Flair is doing the unexpected successfully. It is the art of effective decision-making. However, flair can be acquired on the training field, if players really understand the game and the opportunities presented by turnover ball.

Very effective and well-organized chases from precise kicks limit opportunities for counter-attack by the back three. Counter-attack opportunities are more likely to come from poor or loose kicks. The following principles must be appreciated and understood by the whole team:

- If a counter-attack is to be successful, there must be time, space and support.
- A positive approach should be adopted. For reasons of safety, some sides will counter-attack only in the 15m channel, where it is possible, if things go wrong, to run into touch with the ball or to kick the ball into touch.
- Good communication and decision-

making are vital. If the ball is in the air or on the ground, the player who is fielding it will find it difficult to scan for space simultaneously. One of the other back-three players should slot in behind the fielder and communicate information and decisions – pass, kick high, kick to touch, catch and run forwards, and so on.

- The ball should be brought forwards as quickly as possible, and the players should avoid getting caught behind the majority of their team. They must also aim to reduce the space between the ball and their own forwards quickly. It may be a long way to go back, if things break down, and it is no good playing about while the opposition are coming up fast.
- The ball gatherer ought to off-load the ball to a player who is running, so that the counter-attack can gather pace. A player picking up the ball or receiving a high kick may have lost momentum. The opposition will also be homing in on the ball gatherer, and it may be possible to outflank these players by popping the ball up to a looping player or by giving a wide clearing pass.
- Dummy to strength – in other words, the ball can be taken back in the direction of the kick to check the opposition forwards.
- The attack must be aimed at the biggest space with the fewest

defenders and the ball must be moved to the open areas. If it is necessary to move the ball across the middle of the field, it must be done quickly. A player in midfield running with the ball will get caught if the opposition have been chasing up properly. Midfield players must get back to support, between the ball and their own goal-line.

- The kick can also be a powerful and positive counter-attack tool.

Counter-Attack Opportunities

There are various situations that present a team with counter-attack opportunities in most games. It is usual to create a framework for a counter-attack by the back three. The pattern of movement that emerges largely depends on which player gathers the ball – Open-Side Wing, Full Back or Blind-Side Wing. The organization of the counter-attack is designed to let those involved understand what the ball carrier intends to do and how to play off him.

For the back three, opportunities usually arise from opponents kicking badly in certain areas of the game and typical movement patterns in counter-attack will follow. There must also, however, be an option for an individual player to run hard with his head up, as well as an option of giving an early pass and supporting. This results in two types of counter-attack: the direct, in which one player takes the attack single-handed to the opposition, not worrying about support until later, or kicks; and the indirect, in which the player who gains possession acts in a pivotal role and either passes immediately, or fixes one or more opponents before releasing the ball to the support.

Inside own 22, but, despite support arriving, the decision is to go for territory with the end-over-end kick.

RECEIVING KICK FROM DEFENSIVE LINE-OUT

- The ball is kicked straight to the Full Back. FB immediately runs towards the kicker and the forwards to fix them and switches with 11 (Blind-Side Wing), who heads for the thinly defended right side of the pitch. 12 and 13 work hard to get outside and behind 11 and 14 (Open-Side Wing), who keeps the width

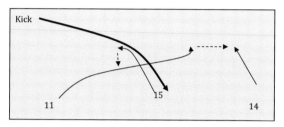

- 15 executes a wiper kick right to the thinly defended area. It is important that there is a positive chase from the kicking side as the kick may not go into touch and can then be potential possession when the defence is outnumbered.

The ball is kicked to the BSW
11 throws a long pass to FB.

- FB angles back towards the kicker and BSW receives a switch pass from FB, if time allows. 11 can then pass to the OSW, short or long ball. 15 must assess the situation in front and may decide to run immediately hard and positively to the space.

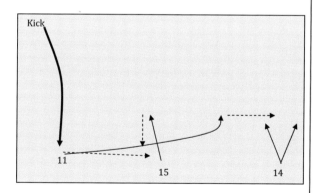

- Two long passes from 11 to 15 to 14 could present attacking, scoring opportunities. 14 can cut back to the defending forwards, hold them in and use runners who have got outside him during the two passes.

Continued overleaf

133

Continued from page 133

Ball kicked to OSW

- 14 should attack the space straight in front, with the others picking up good support lines. Another option could be 14 running back towards the source to dummy switch with FB and switch with BSW. Time may be short!

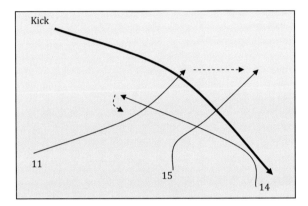

RECEIVING KICK FROM DEFENSIVE SCRUM
(Example scrum on left side of pitch)

- From a scrum on the attacking side's right, the box kick may be used by the Scrum Half. This is difficult for counter-attack as securing the ball has to be the priority before anything else is contemplated. Once the ball is secured, a high kick could be the best option to get the pressure back on the defence, but holding and recycling must be the initial priority.
- The ball is kicked long to 15. This presents 15 with various running line options as there is more actual space for the counter-attack than from a lineout. The line can be anywhere in front but certain principles must be remembered.
- If the run is straight ahead or left, 11 must become a support runner.
- 12 and 13 must work to get back behind 15 to be available as support.
- 15 may decide that the bomb kicking option is the most appropriate counter-attack

Direct: The Lone Runner

If there is an opportunity to run and the decision is taken to do so, the ball carrier should move forwards at pace and at space. If the fielder catches the ball, there will be more time available to take decisions than if the ball has to be retrieved on the ground. There will be space between defenders and behind them. The ball carrier must, at least, get beyond the first line of chasers; he must,

therefore, have good evasive skills. If the contact has to be taken, the ball carrier must fight to stay upright, allowing time for support to get back and secure possession

Indirect: The Pass

The Kick

The decision to kick is based on the need to gain territory. Field position and where space

Activity: Kick and chase

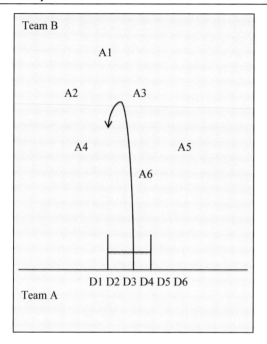

- From under the posts, a player from Team A kicks ball to attackers.
- Team B must bring ball back to score anywhere on goal-line.
- Team A sends one player to defend (two-handed holding tackles).
- Teams swap around, if defending team stops the counter-attack.
- If attacking team is successful and scores a try, defending team kick again and 2 defenders chase.
- If attacking team scores again, another kick takes place with 3 defenders, and so on.

Development:
- Allow re-gain kicks.

Key learning points

Receiving team:

Technical:
- catching under pressure; passing – long pass, switch and loop passes; running – speed over ground, footwork to beat defenders; support – width and depth, communication with ball carrier.

Sequence of play:
- call for the ball; reaction of support players; catch the ball; assess the opposition chase, then attack space.

Key factors:
- be positive; fielder is not the decision-maker; support player gets in behind fielder and takes decisions. If receiver catches cleanly and is running at pace, there is no need for this information.
- Keep the ball off ground.
- Bring the ball forward with pace.
- Support runner to time run when fielder can offer pass.
- Continually transfer focus of attack to keep defenders on move.

Kick and chase:
- quick chase; move up talking in a straight line

is available will be important factors in this decision. In the defensive 22-m zone a player will kick from counter-attack to get the ball off the pitch so that the team can regroup, with everyone behind the ball. Preferably, the ball is kicked into the stand so a quick lineout cannot be taken by the opposition.

If the intention of the kick is to gain territory while keeping the ball on the pitch and encouraging the opposition to kick or run back, the targeted area will be close to the touch-lines. The kick will have a low trajectory to make it harder to catch the ball on the run. The chasing defence form a flat defensive line and close down the retriever's options.

Another option is a re-gain kick, which might be a high ball, a box kick, a cross-field kick or a chip kick. These will be executed in the opposition half. The risk with these is that, if the ball is not recovered, the team will be left vulnerable to a counter-attack themselves.

Measuring success

The criteria for measuring the success of a counter-attack are:

- Did we cross the advantage line?
- Did we keep possession?

Defending

Framework

The vulnerability of the wing, so far from the source of possession, makes defence specifics crucial. Mistakes inside can be covered, but they are much more difficult to cover on the flanks. This begins at set pieces and players have to have some framework to which to work. The Blind-Side Wing and 15 have to split the back field. The Blind-Side Wing stays 15m infield at lineouts rather than taking up a position on the touch-line. This allows the Full Back a central role and the other wing a wide role. Once the ball goes beyond the attacking 10, the Open-Side Wing moves forward to tackle, 15 moves wider and the Blind-Side Wing covers at a shallow angle and inside the ball. A good understanding of the principles of whatever defensive system – for example, drift or blitz – is being employed is vital, as is having a good communication strategy to make changes to defensive patterns as play changes.

Defensive positioning at the scrum is more difficult for the wing and the overriding thought has to be to cover space, rather than numbers. When there is a scrum near the touch-line, the Blind-Side Winger has to cover for any blind-side action, then cover behind the scrum to allow 15 to take a wider position. With a midfield scrum and a split defence, both wings should stay back for a high kick, then move up as the ball goes across the attack's line. Usually, 15 takes a central position, although he can move one way or the other, after the ball is put into the scrum, which can often mislead the kicker.

Pendulum Cover Defence

When playing a four-up defence (the Open-Side Wing up in line with the centres), the Full Back plays up and out, getting ahead of the ball and closer to the touch-line. The Blind-Side Wing covers across when the play goes open. Communication among the back three is essential.

When play is in midfield, both wingers drop back and position themselves slightly infield but ready to field any kicks. If the opposition then moves the ball wide to the right-hand side, the right winger moves forwards level with the centre. The left winger covers across behind the Full Back. If the opposition attacks the left flank, the left winger will move up level and the right winger will cover.

Exercise 1:

- Each team has five attempts at attacking and five at defensive plays.
- There is a four-up defence – the acting Full Back slides across and Blind-Side Winger pushes across and behind.
- A score from tactical kick = 4 points; from a pass = 1 point.
- Sweeper talks to front defenders throughout. Communication is vital.

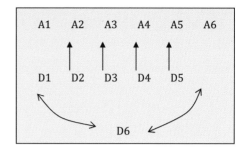

CHAPTER 9

DEVELOPING BACKLINE PLAY

There are two kinds of decision that players must make in rugby: strategic and tactical.

Strategic Decision-Making

The strategic decisions are those where a player has time to decide. This usually follows a refereeing decision, after which the pack leader calls a move from the scrum, the Hooker decides where to throw in the lineout, the Fly Half decides where to make the first strike in the backs, and so on. These decisions are based on the game plan – objectives decided before the match, which continue to evolve during the match, according to the weather conditions or the opposition providing unexpected resistance in the areas being attacked. Often, the coach calls the moves and patterns from the side-line.

Much of a squad's training revolves around team or unit moves and sequences. Coaches

A Mismatch: a Centre against Prop.

The prop cannot cope with the extra pace of the threequarter.

And he is away.

use sequencing so that players know what is happening from a set play while the other team does not. This allows for economy of player movement. Players know where they have to move to and what is happening over first phase (a starter move) and several secondary phases (continuity moves). A sequence involves pre-planning a pattern of moves, and does not allow the players to make decisions for themselves by reacting to the situation in front of them.

Coaches can have immediate success with youth teams by being highly organized. Team success may be good for the reputation of the coach and enjoyable for the players involved, however, there are real doubts about whether it is correct to focus on team rather than individual development. This may not be the best way to produce self-regulating players with good game awareness and, perhaps, international potential. Learning how to win is of course a part of player development, but it is far more important to guide players to develop technically, tactically, physically and mentally, to teach them sound values and to develop character. Players will develop sound tactical sense if they play rugby in an environment that encourages them to recognize space and to use it creatively and effectively. The less cluttered their mind is with having to remember sequences, the more they will be able to focus on and react to what they see in front of them. Sequencing should be used only with care and with an understanding of the issues involved. This is as relevant to a senior player as it is to the young one.

Instinctive Decision-Making

It is possible to over-coach players. Prescriptive, drill-based coaching may improve skills levels, but players coached in this way often have little understanding of when or how best to use these skills. In order to overcome a well-organized defence, players need good decision-making, which can be achieved only if the player can read the situation and react to all the aural and visual clues. Any player in possession of the ball has to decide whether to run, to take the ball into contact, to pass, or to kick the ball. These are spontaneous, instinctive decisions and are determined by the situation and by the player's ability. These decisions are learned by constantly being put into match situations and having to react.

Drills have a place in a training session in developing technique. A skill is a technique successfully performed under pressure, so, by manipulating the time, space and opposition within drills, skills can also be improved. By observing the principle of progression – from simple to complex, unopposed to opposed – drills can be moved closer to game conditions. However, while drills are excellent for using available space for training, and ensuring high levels of activity for a large number of players, they are often organized in isolation, for their own sake rather than being designed for purpose. Coaches tend to instruct and give feedback and players are not encouraged to think for themselves. Due to the repetitive nature of drills, they can also become boring for the players.

Drills should be put into context. Through a game-centred approach and a whole-part-whole philosophy, it is possible to create an active learning environment. Players enjoy playing games and, by playing games, their understanding of the game and their tactical awareness improve. By intervening and extracting a dominant skill from the game and putting it into a drill format, it is possible to refine the parts of the whole. It can then be put back into a game.

Rugby Netball

Organization

- Field 60 x 40m; 2 x goals 10m wide.
- One team starts with the ball and all players attack the other goal, passing the ball between them and attempting to throw the ball through the goal.
- Other team defends with one player retreating to goalkeeper position.
- No running with the ball.
- Any type of pass is allowed.
- Play continues until the ball is dropped, a player is touched in possession of ball or a goal is scored. When any of these occur, the ball is left on the ground and the other team attacks, with the goalkeeper joining in
- Game continues until either a time or goal limit is reached.

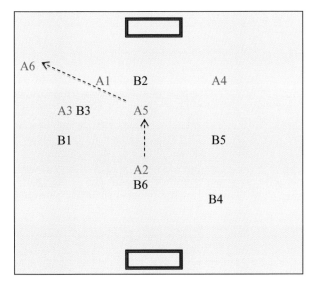

Relevance to the Game

- Working off the ball, getting into space, away from defender, using side-steps, twists, changes of pace.
- Understanding the need to go forwards.
- Clear communication, using aural or visual (hand signals).
- Development of reaction speed, peripheral vision and anticipation, accurate passing in traffic, spatial awareness, footwork.

Off-Load Touch

Organization

- When the ball carrier is touched, an off-load must take place immediately.
- Coach conditions this (for example, for a count of 3 seconds).

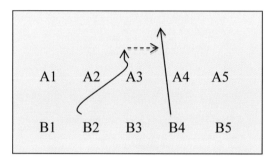

Relevance to the Game

- Development of following skills: spatial awareness, scanning, decision-making, communication, evasion, supporting ball carrier.
- Highlights the importance of getting behind the defence, keeping possession and finishing.
- Support is key for keeping possession alive, with the touched player having to pass immediately and the support runner attacking the ball.
- Change of speed and direction to beat defender.

The Development of Game Understanding

Challenges: 'A bump in the road is either an obstacle to be fought, or an opportunity to be enjoyed…it's all up to you.' Anon

Traditionally, rugby training sessions have been dominated by a coach, with players being told where to stand, how to defend a situation, and so on. The emphasis with the game-sense approach is on the players making decisions rather than the coach. The

Mismatch Touch

Organization

- Normal touch rules.
- Ruck touch (ball presented on ground through legs).
- Two defenders (depending on numbers) wear different coloured bibs. Their touches do not count as a tackle.

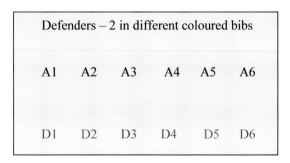

Relevance to the Game

- Scanning for mismatches (for example, a back against a forward, a big player against a smaller one, a faster player against a slower one).
- Scanning for space.
- Attackers look before receiving ball to move to a good position in which to receive the ball.
- Communication comes from the outside players to the inside players if a mismatch or space is seen.
- Weak defenders to stay away from each other and in areas that are highly congested with other defenders (close to the contact area).

coach's role is that of a facilitator, aiming to create self-autonomous athletes – players who can think out solutions for themselves, which is far more effective for long-term learning than being told what to do.

A coach can none the less ask questions of the player, in order to aid understanding and promote tactical thinking: 'Why did you take that decision?', 'Why did you pass when you did?', 'Where is the best spot to stand?', 'Where will it be more difficult for your opponent to score from?' By going through the cues that the mind has processed to make the various decisions, a coach can help the player decide which ones were important and

which were less important. The key factors to focus on are visual information (what the player sees) and aural information (the calls from team-mates).

Before asking questions such as these, the coach must be able to create a situation or game in which problem-solving can take place. Games already exist in rugby. It is easy enough to create games out of drills to emphasize the tactical aspects. The key is to design a game in which the players have the opportunity to practise what is relevant in the real game. In practical terms, a coach using a game-sense will modify the practice, with a view to exaggerating or emphasizing particular tactical aspects. Such modifications might include changes to the dimensions of the practice area, to the number of passes allowed, to the number of players in attack and defence; he might give penalty or bonus points for particular plays or he may vary the time allowed for particular drills. Rules can be added to or removed from the game as it increases in complexity.

The game-sense approach has a number of benefits for both the coach and the player. Coaches may find that it challenges some of the traditional ways they have been taught to coach. However, they may well find that the coaching process and the games themselves are more challenging for themselves and for their players.

Support Touch

Organization

- Area 30 x 30m.
- When the attacking player touched, he scoops the ball through the legs.
- If a supporting player does not catch the ball before it hits the ground, it is turnover ball.

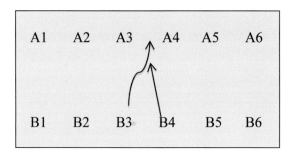

Relevance to the Game

- Importance of players supporting the ball carrier.
- Encourages players to attack the ball at pace and get close to the ball carrier.
- Supporting players attack the ball (usually the player who last passed the ball – pass and support).
- Importance of possession and team continuity.
- Encourages development of the following skills: spatial awareness, communication, decision-making, attacking space.
- Change of speed and direction to beat defenders.
- Emphasis on getting behind the defence and producing quick ball.

Games with an Attacking Emphasis

Counter-Attack Game

Organization

- A number is called for the attackers. All attackers run around the numbered cone and the ball relating to the number that was called becomes active.
- At the same time a colour is called for the defenders and all defenders must turn and run around the nominated coloured cone.
- If a touch is made, players swap roles. If a try is scored, attackers stay the same.
- First to five wins.

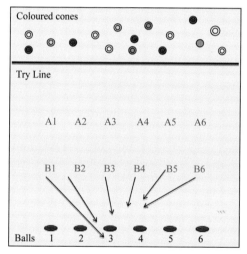

Relevance to the Game

- Counter-attacking unorganized defences.
- Speed of attack.
- Attacking space.
- Decision-making in identifying space and the best way to attack it successfully.
- Development of following skills: communication, spatial awareness, passing, decision-making, evasion.

Number Touch

Organization

- Area 30 × 30m.
- Players are given numbers.
- When an attacking team is about to start an attack, numbers are called and nominated defenders go to knees and take no part in the game.
- When play breaks down or another touch is made, nominated defenders are back in the game.

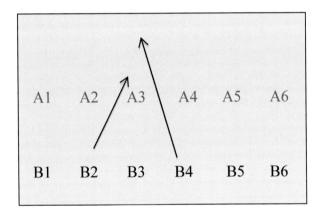

Relevance to the Game

- Scanning quickly to identify defenders who are out of the game, creating space and mismatches (more against fewer, fast against slow).
- Attacking an unorganized defence (counter-attack).
- These situations occur at turnovers, rucks and tackle areas in the game where the attacking team might find forwards in the backs' defensive line.
- Promotes attacking spaces, spatial awareness, decision-making, communication, evasion.

Colours Touch

Organization

- Area 30 x 30m.
- Each player is given a colour.
- When the attacking team is mounting an attack, if a colour is called, all defensive players with that colour run around the nearest cone of that colour.
- For conditioning and realignment purposes all players can run around an allotted cone colour.
- Coach must have two rugby balls to ensure a fast game and a change of defence to attack at times.

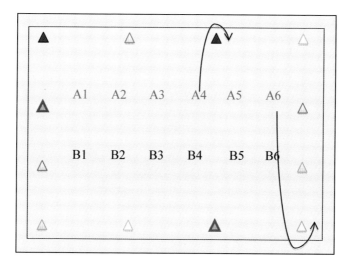

Relevance to the Game

- Excellent for speed of perception and counter-attacking, identifying spaces created by the leaving defenders.
- Promotes identification and attacking of space, as well as communication (highlighting spaces and mismatches) and handling.
- Decision-making on how to attack the space.

Games with a Defensive Emphasis

Man-on-Man Touch

Organization

- Normal two-handed touch rules apply.
- Unlimited touches are allowed.
- If touched, the player must pass immediately.
- Players in attack and defence are paired up – 1 with 1, 2 with 2, and so on.
- Defenders can only touch the attacking player with whom they are paired.
- If the ball is dropped, it should be left on the ground and the other team attacks.
- When a try is scored, the defender who was marking the player who scored must get the ball quickly and begin attacking the far try-line.
- When allocating partners, the coach can initially allocate players of equal speed and agility, or deliberately create mismatches.
- If there are unequal numbers, the player without a partner can roam and defend against any player – in other words, play as a Full Back.
- The game can be developed by varying the field size, or changing partners after a try is scored or a mistake occurs.

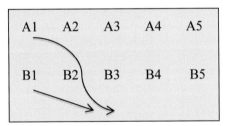

Relevance to the Game

- Highlights the importance of working off the ball and anticipating where to defend (scramble back defence) and where to attack (supporting ball carrier).
- Reaction speed, to turn defence into attack quickly or change attacking mentality into defensive, if ball lost.
- Conditioning: speed endurance, with shorts bursts followed by brief jogging recovery periods.
- Development of agility and evasive skills.

Drift Touch

Organization

- Area 60 × 40m.
- Teams of four in different-coloured bibs, more attackers than defenders.
- Defenders always start in a coned area.
- Bib colour called, that team becomes the defending team, starting in coned area.
- Game starts with Scrum Half (with supply of balls) passing to either group left or right.
- Defenders then leave tackle area and defend try-line.
- Defenders can only defend laterally.
- Attackers get one chance to score. If this is achieved the Scrum Half passes a ball to another group of attackers and defenders must move across to defend them.
- The Scrum Half can pass when a try is scored, a touch is made or the ball is dropped.
- The winning team is the one conceding the lowest number of tries.

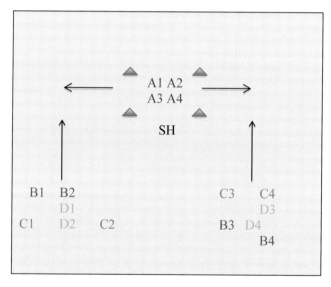

Relevance to the Game

- Development of the drift defence.
- Angles of running and movement on to the ball to beat a drift defence.
- Support lines – attacking in two waves.
- Development of following skills: spatial awareness, communication in attack and defence, decision-making, attacking space, conditioning.
- Both attack and defence are working off the ball.

Double-Touch

Organization

- Field dimensions: half-field.
- Same rules as two-handed touch except the ball carrier must be touched twice before stopping to play the ball.
- Play continues until the ball carrier is touched twice, the ball is dropped, or a try is scored.

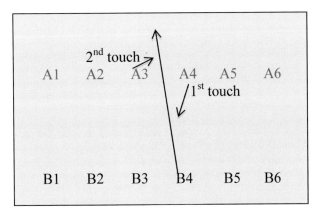

Relevance to the Game

- The aim is to ensure that inside defenders stay alive in defence once their immediate opponent has passed the ball.
- Defenders align on inside shoulder of immediate opponent.
- Defensive agility – players should not plant their feet laterally; the defender must be aligned with the outside foot up, nominating and pointing at the attacker they are marking, on the toes, not the heels. The defender must move quickly off line when half moves the ball, tracking the hip of their opposite number.
- All defenders on the inside of the ball carrier to remain in line and also to push to the ball.
- When the ball carrier moves the ball wide, the immediate defender must push directly to the new ball carrier.
- Inside defenders do not run behind the defensive line, getting past ball, as this will open up the blind side for the attack to exploit.
- Defenders working off the ball.

Drift or Blitz Touch

Organization

- 30 x 30m grid.
- Within a game of touch, the coach can, at any breakdown, call 'blitz' or 'drift' and the defenders have to run and touch the appropriate line.
- The coach can also have more attackers versus fewer defenders by numbering each player and nominating players to leave the game. When their number is called, the players run to the side-line and take no part in subsequent play.
- Attackers must face the other way and attack when the ball is rolled behind them. The closest attacker picks up.

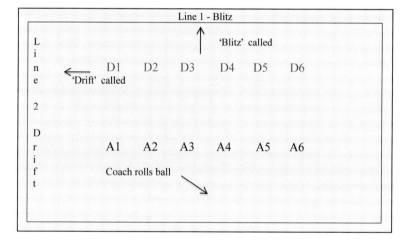

Relevance to the Game

- Attacking differing defensive alignments and doing so appropriately.
- Encouraging attackers to identify spaces created by leaving defenders, deciding on the appropriate action, and attacking the space.
- Promotes communication and handling.

Games With A Kicking Emphasis

Kick-Pass Game

Organization

- Whole or modified field with a goalmouth at either end.
- The aim is to kick the ball between the posts, scoring a goal.
- Passes are made by kicking the ball to other team members, using any type of kick.
- Defenders cannot charge down kicks but can compete for the ball in the air and on the ground.
- Any player can act as goalkeeper.

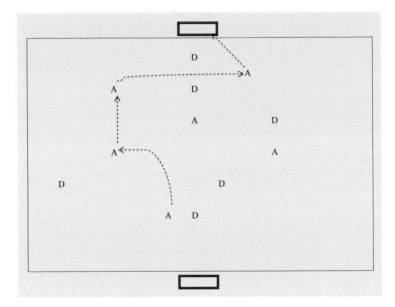

Relevance to the Game

- Emphasis on accuracy of kicking and choice of correct kick (grubber, chip, spiral or end-over-end punt).
- Development of the skills of fielding kicks in the air and on the ground and under pressure from a defender.

Kick-Score Game

Organization

- Normal rules of touch rugby.
- If scoring a try from a pass, the team gets 1 point.
- If scoring from a kick, the team gets 5 points.

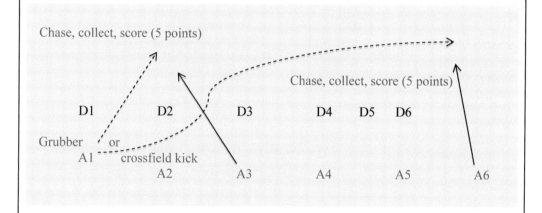

Relevance to the Game

- Scoring from accurate tactical kicks.
- Appropriateness of choice of kick.
- Counter-attacks from kick receipt.

GLOSSARY OF TECHNICAL TERMS

Body position   The height at which contact is initiated.

Body shape   The physical positioning of the body skeleton.

Change of angle   Ability to change the direction of run.

Change of pace   Ability to speed up or slow down.

Chip kick   A short lofted kick.

Clear out   Moving defenders backwards from the ball in a ruck.

Clearing pass   A long fast spiral pass away from a group of players.

Cut-out pass   A long pass intended to 'miss out' a team-mate.

Fixing the defender   Forcing the defender to commit to a tackle.

Drop kick   Kick executed after the ball has touched the ground.

Dummy   A faked pass where the ball does not leave the hands.

Fend/hand-off   Creating space through physical contact with the opponent with an outstretched arm.

Formation   The arrangement of players performing a particular function.

Grubber   Kick in which the ball 'dribbles' along the ground.

Inside pass   A pass in the direction from which the ball was received.

Lateral pass   Basic, fundamental or orthodox rugby pass.

Penetration   Ability to exploit gaps in the defence, or to drive through the defensive line.

Place kick   Kick executed when the ball is stationary on the ground.

Pop pass   A two-handed lofted pass.

Position   Reference to the specific role of an individual player.

Positioning – depth   Location of support player behind the ball carrier.

Positioning – width   Location of support player beside the ball carrier.

Punt   A long high kick for distance.

Realignment   Reorganization of players who are about to attack with the ball, or defend.

Side-step   A quick lateral step.

Speed of delivery   The rate at which the ball is produced from set pieces and loose play.

Step over   Taking the space between the ball and the defenders.

Swerve   Long lateral change in direction while running.

Switch pass   A short pass facing the receiver who is running at an angle to the ball carrier.

Tap kick   A quick kick by the player to himself, to restart play.

Up and under   A high kick with little distance.

Wiper kick   A long, driving kick.

INDEX

RELATED TITLES
FROM CROWOOD

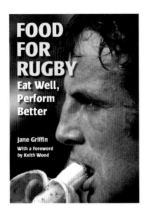

Food for Rugby
East Well, Perform Better

Jane Griffin

ISBN 978 1 86126 695 8
128pp, 25 illustrations

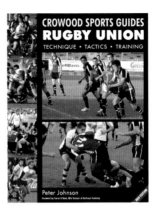

Rugby Union
Crowood Sports Guide

Peter Johnson

ISBN 978 1 84797 064 0
128pp, 200 illustrations

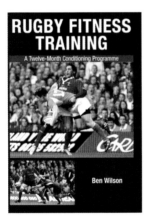

Rugby Fitness Training
A Twelve-Month Conditioning Programme

Ben Wilson

ISBN 978 1 86126 850 1
192pp, 170 illustrations

Rugby Training

Stuart Biddle, Barrie Corless, Anne de Looy,
Peter Thomas

ISBN 978 1 85223 897 1
128pp, 100 illustrations

In case of difficulty ordering, contact the Sales Office:

The Crowood Press
Ramsbury
Wiltshire
SN8 2HR
UK

Tel: 44 (0) 1672 520320
enquiries@crowood.com
www.crowood.com